SOCIAL FUNDRAISING

ARVIND UPADHYAY

This book is designed to help small organizations raise money effectively by building a broad base of individual donors. But private-sector giving cannot take the place of government funding, and the nonprofit sector cannot solve the many social problems created or exacerbated by public policies more commonly associated with oligarchies than democracies. Nonetheless, an organization that is financed by a broad base of individual donors is in the strongest position to advocate for the structural changes our society must make. The late management guru Peter Drucker said, "Every important idea for social change has come from the nonprofit sector." For these ideas to become reality, they must be supported by the time and money of dozens, hundreds, or thousands of people. For organizations serious about social change, the number of donors you have is as important as the amount of money you raise, and to state the obvious, the more donors you have, the more money you will raise. In this book, I assume you are already working as hard as you can; I suggest ways for you to work smarter. Then you can find and reach the donors you need to get the money you deserve. This is a how-to book. Its goal is to provide organizations that have budgets of less than two million dollars (including much less than that) with the information they need to establish, maintain, and expand a successful community-based fundraising program. Building a broad base of individual donors gives organizations maximum freedom to pursue their mission. They can then use foundation, corporate, or government grants for special programs, start-up costs, technical assistance, capital or endowment projects, or other time-limited needs. Organizations with small budgets, particularly those working for social change, need to keep in mind that the context in which their fundraising efforts take place is different from that of large, established organizations such as universities. First, the name of your group is not a household word. And even when they hear about you, many people will not understand what you are trying to do. Many of those who do understand may disagree with you, particularly if you are trying to challenge the status quo. Even those in sympathy with your mission may think your aims are hopelessly naïve or idealistic; you may often be told to "face reality." Second, you probably have little or no front money and not enough staff and you are often either just holding your own financially or falling behind. Third, your board of directors, volunteers, and staff are likely to be unfamiliar with fundraising strategies and may not be comfortable with the idea of asking for money. For grassroots groups such as yours, traditional fundraising strategies need to be rethought and *translated into workable terms. This book does that. All of the strategies explained and recommended here have been successful for small groups. Not every strategy will work for every group, but the discussion of each strategy will allow you to decide which strategies will work for your group and how to expand the strategies you are already using. Fundraising without planning, without a strong, committed group of volunteers to help, without a workable organizational structure, or without understanding the basic components of all fundraising plans is practically impossible. The appropriate staff, whether paid or unpaid, of every organization should read the first two sections of this book to learn the context for successful fundraising. The next sections present detailed descriptions of how to carry out strategies to acquire, retain, and upgrade donors to your organization. These proceed from the most impersonal—direct mail appeals and special events—to the most personal—solicitation by telephone and in person. The book gives special attention to the difficulties most people have asking for money and offers concrete ways to overcome these difficulties. Finally, the book covers how to create a budget and a fundraising plan and the rudiments of setting up a fundraising office, keeping records, working with an executive director, and hiring fundraising staff or consultants. Special circumstances for fundraising are also discussed, such as raising money in rural communities or raising money for a coalition of groups. There are many fundraising strategies that are not covered in this book, and readers are encouraged to explore them. However, all successful fundraising strategies are, at the end of the day, about people. Corporate giving is about knowing someone in the corporation who will shepherd your cause through their system. Service clubs, houses of worship, foundations, and so on are also about knowing someone. So even though this book doesn't cover that specifically, it does cover what you need to know to pursue any strategy you want to pursue. If you find this book helpful, I encourage you to buy my other books and to subscribe to the Grassroots Fundraising Journal, a bimonthly publication that will help you keep up with fundraising strategies and developments in the field. I also encourage you to buy my training videotapes and use them with your board. All that helps me, and it will help you. But ultimately, after you have read about how to raise money and gone to workshops on how to do it, the only thing left is to do it. Like driving a car or learning to swim, all the theory and explanation will not help until you get behind the wheel or into the pool and try it for yourself. Few people give money without being asked. Make this your motto:*

"Today somebody has to ask somebody for money."

Contents

1

United States in Philanthropy

The word philanthropy comes from two Greek words meaning "love of people." In modern times this goodwill, or humanitarianism, is often expressed in donations of property, money, or volunteer time to worthy causes. Similarly, the word charity comes from a Latin word meaning "love" in the sense of unconditional lovingkindness, compassion, and seeking to do good. The roots of these words remind us of the fundamental reasons for the work of most nonprofit organizations. The United States has the largest system of organized private philanthropy in the world. In this country, nongovernmental organizations have been created— and funded through private sources—to provide services that countries with greater government commitment to social welfare provide directly and fund through taxation. If nonprofits in the United States were a single industry, they would rank as the nation's largest industry, accounting for just under 10 percent of the workforce and about 5 percent of the gross domestic product. As of 2005, more than 1.5 million organizations have been recognized by the Internal Revenue Service as tax exempt. Several million more small, grassroots organizations that are doing important charitable work are not registered with the government and have no formal tax status. These groups include organizations just getting started; organizations using a fiscal sponsor; organizations that use very little money, such as neighborhood block clubs; organizations that come together for a one-time purpose, such as cleaning up a vacant lot or protesting something; and those that don't wish to have a structural relationship with the state or federal government. Because of the size and growing sophistication of the nonprofit sector, it has increasingly drawn the attention of the government, researchers, academics, and many members of the general public. Although nonprofits are increasingly regulated by federal, state, and local government, public awareness, coupled with the role of individuals in funding *nonprofits, means that voluntary compliance with accepted ethical standards of accounting, personnel, and fundraising practice provides an added, and usually sufficient, layer of self-regulation. Nonprofit status is a public trust and tax exemption is, in effect, a public expense. Even if an organization has no formal tax status, if it seeks to raise money from the public it has the same moral duty as registered nonprofits to operate ethically, be truthful with donors, and provide the highest quality of services to clients. THE FOUNDATION-CORPORATE GIVING MYTH As with many endeavors that are critically important and use the resources of millions of people, it is not surprising that a number of misconceptions have grown up about philanthropy and charities. The most serious misconception for fundraising is many people's belief that most money given to nonprofits comes from foundations and corporations. The truth is far different. Of all the income of all nonprofits, about half is earned income: fees for service, tuition, products for sale, and the like. About 30 percent of nonprofit income is derived from government programs (collectively known as "the public sector"). Extensive cutbacks in government funding starting in the 1980s and continuing to this day have reduced government funding a great deal, but it remains a significant source of income for many organizations. The final 20 percent of nonprofit income is from the private sector: individuals, foundations, and corporations. For most of the organizations using this book, the private sector will provide the majority of your funding. Surprising to most people is the fact that gifts from individuals make up the bulk of private-sector funding, far more than all foundation and corporate money combined. This book focuses almost entirely on how to raise money from that enormous market of individual donors. There is now an enormous body of research on philanthropy, both in the United States and in other countries, and determining who gives what to whom and why comprises a lot of it. The most widely used report is Giving USA, compiled yearly by the Giving USA Foundation AAFRC Trust for Philanthropy. Every year since 1935, the authors have calculated just how much money was given away to nonprofits and by whom. They have identified four general sources of gifts from the private (nongovernmental) sector: living individuals, bequests (cash or other donations an individual arranges to be given to a charity on their death), foundations, and corporations. Their research shows that the proportion of giving from each of these sources remains constant, varying from year to year by only two or three percentage points, with gifts from individuals (living or deceased) exceeding the rest by an impressive ratio of nine to one. For the year 2005, the latest for which figures are available, giving from these sources totaled $260.68 billion.*

WHO GIVES AWAY MONEY? The logical follow-up question—Who are these people?—is more difficult to answer because there are many complex variables. Not only does the answer vary by which methods are used in doing the research, but there are also many aspects of giving that it is difficult for researchers to learn about. The bottom line is that, although the Giving USA figures presented above are probably fairly accurate in terms of foundation and corporate giving—which is easier to measure—giving by individuals is probably even greater than those statistics can measure. Here's why. There are some formal ways that estimates of individual giving are made: by analyzing the tax returns of people who itemize their giving and extrapolating from them, by surveying a random sample of the population about their giving and extrapolating from their answers, and by comparing the results of either or both of these methods with what charities report of their income, either in their own tax filing statements (known by the name of the IRS form, 990) or in polls and surveys. The data collected in any of these ways can then be further analyzed by demographic breakdowns, such as the age or income of the donor, or by looking Sources of Contributions, 2004 Contributions From Amount in Billions Percentage of Total Individuals $187.92 75.6 Bequests $19.80 8.0 Foundations $28.80 11.6 Corporations $12.00 4.8 Source: Giving USA, 2006. at the giving patterns of a particular set of donors over several years. Further information can be learned by comparing the characteristics of donors with those of nondonors or by conducting focus groups on why (and to what) people give or don't give. There are a few well-known, established sources of research on who gives away money, how much, and to what. Perhaps the best known is Giving USA, cited above. Independent Sector, a leadership forum for nonprofits that also reports on giving in the United States, publishes a biannual report, Giving and Volunteering in the USA, based on written and phone surveys. The Center on Philanthropy at Indiana University surveys giving and volunteering by the same households over time as families and reports its findings in its Center on Philanthropy Panel Study (known as COPPS). Other researchers include the Center on Wealth and Philanthropy at Boston College, the Foundation Center, the National Center for Charitable Statistics, the NewTithing Group, and empty tomb, inc. (for research on religion). Each of these institutions uses slightly different methods of counting philanthropic giving, with correspondingly disparate results. No matter what method is used, however, chances are that charitable giving by individuals is underreported because of the limitations of the information available. For research that uses tax returns to estimate giving, as with Giving USA, it's important to note that only 30 percent of Americans file an itemized return. The 70 percent of Americans who file a "short form" receive *no tax benefits from their giving because their giving doesn't exceed the standard deduction. Extrapolating what nonitemizers give is done with an econometric model. Though there is no reason to think the results from this model are wildly inaccurate, the estimates are probably conservative and thereby likely undercount a lot of giving. For those who do report giving on their tax forms, we are confronted with the fact that people tend to understate their income and exaggerate their giving. By how much? Hard to say. When people are surveyed by phone about their giving, might they exaggerate their generosity? Probably. By how much? Hard to say. Certainly, people often forget how much they have given to charity when they have no incentive, such as a tax deduction, to help them remember. Possibly the exaggerators cancel out the underreporters. Add to that mix that rules about what is tax deductible and what is not are confusing even to nonprofits, and we can safely assume that it is difficult to say with great accuracy exactly who gives away money and how much they give away every year.Here are some other variables that make knowing who gives away money difficult: Although the majority of people give money from their annual income, the wealthy minority give from their assets. Studies looking at who is generous relative to their ability sometimes only compare income; others look at net worth. These can yield different results. For example, a family could have a low income but be quite wealthy because of assets, or have a low income and be poor. Studies that calculate in which region of the country people are the most generous usually fail to take into account cost of living. For example, compare two states where the median income is $40,000 but in one state the median cost of housing is twice as expensive as in the other. The people living in the first state might well give less money away than those in the other state, but proportionate to their disposable income, they might be equally generous. Almost all studies try to focus on formal philanthropic giving, but if we were to count the amount of money donated to homeless people on the street, or sent as remittances to family members in other countries, or given to help a friend pay for college or to help a poor family pay rent for a few months, not only would our studies show much more giving, they would probably reveal even more demographic differences among givers. Looking at what charities report as their income would seem to give the most accurate data on how much people give to charity, but there are two factors that make this, too, a less reliable source. First, as mentioned, a lot of money donated by individuals doesn't necessarily go to established charities. Second, religious organizations are not required to file 990s (some do voluntarily), so we don't really have an accurate picture of how much income or what the sources of income are for religious institutions. Similarly, organizations with* *budgets of less than $25,000 are also not required to file a 990. For these many organizations, then, we are operating in the realm of guesswork about their total incomes and sources of income. So you can see the problem of trying to learn who gives away money, how much they give, and where it goes: the majority of people do not declare their giving on their tax forms, and a large number of nonprofits are not reporting their income sources. A final compounding factor is that who gives how much away has been changing as the U.S. economy has changed over the past ten years. For many years the bulk of money given away in the United States came from middle-class and working-class people. In 1998, Independent Sector's research showed that about 82 percent of all giving came from households with incomes of $65,000 or less, which was the majority of people. By 2000, the increasing disparity between rich and poor began to show up in giving. The most recent Giving USA notes that households with a gross income of $100,000 or less, which describes 92 percent of all households according to the IRS, contributed only about 52 percent of all giving, whereas households with a net worth of $5 million or more (1 percent of all households) contributed 28 percent of all gifts. Of course, this group also earns more than 40 percent of all income and owns more than 85 percent of all publicly traded stock, so as a group they are not particularly generous. Regardless of how the figures are analyzed, people with smaller household incomes now account for less total giving than they did eight years ago. Giving USA notes, "The trend toward increasing inequality in income in the past two decades paired with different giving patterns to charitable organizations by income level will affect the overall distribution of contributions among nonprofit organizations in the coming years." Further, as United for a Fair Economy— an independent organization that studies and reports on wealth and power in the United States—points out, the wealthy are growing wealthier as the middle-class loses ground. One indicator is the difference in pay between those at the top and those below them. As of 2004, the ratio of what the average CEO is paid (now $11.8 million) to what the average worker is paid (now $27,460) is 431-to-1. (If the minimum wage had risen as fast as CEO pay since 1990, the lowest-paid workers in the United States would be earning $23.03 an hour today instead of their current $5.15 an hour.) The disparities between what lowest-paid and highest-paid workers earn in the United States is the greatest in the world. This situation not only speaks to a need for a more just tax system, it also means that the majority of people do not have much money to contribute. As the gap grows and the middle class becomes smaller, giving by the majority of individuals may go down in actual dollars, even if it doesn't go down as a percentage of income. THE TRUTH ABOUT GIVING Despite the difficulties of learning exactly* *who gives and to what, the following facts are found in a number of studies, they have been found year after year, and they are borne out by the experience of development professionals all over the world. About seven of every ten adults in the United States and Canada give away money. Where these numbers have been studied more locally, we have some interesting variation. For example, in Hawai'i nine out of ten adults give away money; in Alaska, six out of ten do. In Boulder, Colorado, where I grew up, a smaller percentage of the population gives away money than in nearby Denver. More people give away money in Nova Scotia than in British Columbia. (Here's a fun sampling from around the world: in Holland, almost 90 percent of the population gives away money, despite paying very high taxes. In Korea, 64 percent give; in the Philippines, 80 percent.) Middle- and lower-income donors are responsible for a significant percentage of the money given—from 50 to 80 percent—and are the majority of givers. Most people who give to nonprofits give to at least five and as many as fifteen groups. About 20 percent of people on welfare give away money (with the average gift being $74), and about 97 percent of millionaires give away money (Center on Philanthropy data). Volunteers are more likely to be donors than people who don't volunteer. More people give away money than vote. The majority of people who give away money describe themselves as religious or spiritual, whether or not they are involved in a formal religious or spiritual community. And finally, a theme I will return to a thousand times in this book, people give when they are asked. In the United States, the lion's share of private-sector giving, according to all studies, goes to religion. Religious organizations also make up the majority of nonprofits in the United States. Religion has lost market share over the years. When I entered the field of fundraising in 1976, religious giving was 50 percent of all giving; now it is just over 30 percent. Generation X seems to be giving less to religion than previous generations, but that may change as that generation ages.*

Nonetheless, regardless of the methodology used or the variables considered, study after study give us a picture of a generous country, with most people making donations and feeling good about doing so. They also give us a picture of middle- and lower-income donors making up a significant percentage of all money given away and of a constantly increasing amount of money given every year. Foundations and corporations, which have the false reputation of keeping charity alive, are overrated as a source of funds and the help they can provide is often misunderstood. While foundation and corporate giving will always play a vital role in the nonprofit sector, the limitations of that role must be clearly understood. FOUNDATIONS Foundations have relatively little money, and that money is in very great demand. Many of the larger foundations report receiving one hundred proposals for every two they are able to fund. As information about foundations becomes more easily available via the Internet, the demand is increasing. Online databases help potential grantees identify more and more sources. Many foundations now post their guidelines and annual reports on the World Wide Web. Some progressive foundations have adopted a standard grant application form, allowing grantees to submit exactly the same proposal to many different foundations. The very things that thus make foundations more accessible also make them inundated with requests. Although many nonprofits, especially new or small organizations, think foundation funding would be the answer to their money problems, in fact foundation funding is designed to be used only for short-term projects. These include the start up of a new organization and its first few years of operation; capital improvements; new programs; one-time projects, such as studies or conferences; capacity building; or for help through a particularly rough period in the life of an organization for which it has a good excuse and a realistic recovery plan. More recently, foundations have been creating "initiatives," where they focus most or all of their grantmaking on one area of their choosing, such as preschools, youth organizing, or immigrants rights. These initiatives are often helpful for bringing together a number of organizations working on the same issue, allowing them to share ideas and create joint strategies. Sometimes several foundations join an initiative. However, the foundation funding invariably dries up before the problems identified by the initiatives have been solved, leaving groups that have relied heavily on this funding in a bad way. Many foundations, recognizing the limits of their funding, have provided capacity-building grants, which are largely efforts to help organizations move away from the foundation to a more diverse set of income streams. If an organization has come to rely on foundation funding, decreasing reliance should be an important part of its financial planning. If an organization has never become reliant on foundation funding, it should plan not to, and it should not make the mistake common to many small organizations of seeking more foundation funding as the years pass rather than less. CORPORATIONS Corporations are different from foundations in a key way: unlike foundations, whose job is to give money away, corporations exist to make money. Giving money away is primarily an activity that a corporation hopes will directly or indirectly help it to make more money. Even so, only 11 percent of corporations give away any money at all. Moreover, although they are allowed to give away up to 10 percent of their pretax profits, in fact the average amount these companies give away is a mere 1 percent of pretax profits. Corporations that do give money generally give it to the following types of organizations or activities:

· *Organizations that improve the life of the community where their employees live (symphonies, parks, museums, libraries) · Groups that help their employees be more productive by addressing common employee problems (alcohol and drug rehabilitation, domestic violence) · Organizations that provide volunteer opportunities for employees, or to which employees make donations · Research activities that will help the company invent products or market existing products (various departments in universities get much of their funding for such research from corporations) · Education programs for young people to ensure an adequate future workforce for the company (literacy programs, innovative schools, scholarships) More frequent and generous is corporate giving to match employee donations. Although many corporations have had matching gift programs for some time, the scale of today's matching programs have come to be called "employee-driven philanthropy." For this reason it is important to know where your donors work and whether their corporation will match their gift.*

Aside from money, corporations make other valuable donations, such as contributions of expertise (loaning a worker to help a nonprofit with accounting, marketing, or personnel), space (free use of conference or meeting rooms), printing, discarded furniture and office equipment (computers, fax machines, copy machines), building materials, and so on. The past couple of decades have seen many corporations joining with charities in what is called "cause-related marketing" efforts, in which a corporation donates a certain percentage of its profits from a particular item or a certain amount of each sale to its partner charity. The nonprofit group and the corporation advertise the arrangement and encourage people who may be choosing among similar products to choose the one that also benefits the charity. Variations on this theme include corporations that offer to give a percentage of profits to a certain kind of organization (environmental, progressive, feminist) or who allow customers to nominate groups that should receive corporate funding. Cause-related marketing has benefited many organizations by allowing shoppers to feel that their spending can also serve a charitable purpose. The drawback is that these donors do not become part of an organization's donor base, about which much more will be said in the course of this book. Some organizations are not able to get corporate funding because their work is too controversial, others are not located near any corporate headquarters, and others will not seek corporate funding because they wish to avoid appearing to endorse a corporate product or a particular corporation's way of doing business. However, if your group does wish to seek corporate funding, keep in mind that the key element is knowing someone in the corporation. Having "a friend at the bank"—literally and figuratively—is important, and the many ways a corporation can help you should not be overlooked. Just like foundation giving, however, income from corporate giving should not be relied on. THE POWER OF INDIVIDUAL GIVING I hope it is clear by now that a broad base of individual donors provides the only reliable source of funding for a nonprofit year in and year out, and the growth of individual donations to an organization is critical to its growth and self-sufficiency. Further, relying on a broad base of individuals for support increases an organization's ability to be self-determining: it does not need to base program priorities on what foundations, corporations, or government agencies will fund.

Recipients of Charitable Giving To really understand private-sector giving, it is important to look not only at who gives this money, but also at who receives it. Again, with only a few percentage points of variation from year to year, Giving USA has reported a consistent pattern of where gifts go. A little more than one-third of all the money given away in America goes to religious organizations, with education a distant second, followed by health, human services, the arts, and four other categories that receive small percentages of giving.

Giving categorized as "public-society benefit" includes gifts to organizations concerned with community organizing, civil rights, and civil liberties, as well as gifts to United Way, Jewish Federation, and combined funds, such as the Combined Federal Campaign. The category of "gifts to foundations" includes giving to community and private foundations and tends to vary from year to year. Giving to foundations was particularly high in 2005 because of several $1 billion gifts given in the last several years, including $3 billion given by Bill and Melinda Gates to their foundation, and $2.6 billion from the estate of Susan Buffett, both in 2004, and $51 million given for disaster relief.

The category called "unallocated giving" includes deductions carried over, that is, amounts claimed in one year for a gift made up to five years earlier. This situation occurs when charitable contributions exceed 50 percent of a taxpayer's gross adjusted income, when foundations make grants to organizations outside the United States, and most interesting to anyone concerned about privatization, some gifts to government entities. Since they are funded by taxes, government entities that receive private donations, such as public schools, public libraries, public health departments, and the like, are not required to report these gifts. Giving to Religion Religion as a category receives one-third of every charitable dollar, yet only a small percentage of giving to religion is from foundations and virtually none of it is from corporations. Until recently, because of the constitutional separation of church and state, religious activity received little government funding either, except for providing a specific social service. Under a controversial program of President George W. Bush's administration, religious organizations have been able to receive more government funding than in the past. Many religious groups opt not to apply for this money, however, because they do not believe religion should do the work of government; groups that have received such government funding often report that the amounts given are not as much as the controversy would have led the public to believe. Even with this money, it remains true that the vast majority of funding that religious organizations receive is from their own members. We can learn a lot by examining what makes fundraising for religious institutions so successful. At first glance, many people think that religious institutions receive so much money because of their theology: the reward of heaven, the blessing of giving, the threat of eternal damnation for those who do not give. While these enticements may play a role in some people's giving, it is clear that in the wide variety of religious expression, these motives are not enough. Some religious traditions do not believe in any form of eternal life; others don't even believe in God. Even in traditions that encompass some of these beliefs, mature adults can be given more credit than to think that their behavior is based simply on a desire for rewards or a fear of punishment. So why do religious organizations receive almost one-third of all private-sector dollars? Although religious institutions offer ideas and commitments that are of great value, the reason they get money—and this is key to understanding successful fundraising—is that they ask for it. Let's take as an example a Protestant or Catholic church. (If you are of a different religious tradition, compare your own tradition to what follows.) Here is how they raise money: They ask every time worshippers are assembled, which is at least once a week. They make it easy to give: a basket is passed to each person in the service and all gifts are acceptable, from loose change to large checks. Everyone—whether out-of-town visitor, occasional church goer, or loyal and generous congregant— is given the same opportunity to give. The ushers are not concerned about offending someone by asking. They would never say, "Don't pass the basket to Phyllis Frontpew—she just bought the new carpet," or "Skip over Joe because he just lost his job." They make it easy to give, even if you are not a regular congregant. Once a year, most houses of worship will have some kind of stewardship drive or allmember canvass; in many churches, someone will come to your house and ask you how much you will be pledging this year. You can pay your pledge by the week, month, or quarter, or give a one-time gift. The option of pledging and paying over time allows people to give a great deal more over the course of a year than most could in a single lump sum. They provide a variety of programs to which you can give as you desire. If you are particularly interested in the youth program you can give to that, you can buy flowers for the altar, support the music program, or help fund overseas missions. Many churches have scholarships, homeless shelters, food banks, or other social programs. And of course, if you are a "bricks-and-mortar" person, you can contribute to any number of capital improvements—new hymnals, a new window, a better organ, or a whole new sanctuary. Finally, religious institutions approach fundraising with the attitude that they are doing you as much of a favor to ask as you will be doing them to give. In other words, they recognize that fundraising allows an exchange to happen between a person who wants to see a certain kind of work get done and an institution that can do that work. If one of your values and beliefs is that a house of worship is important, then in order for that institution to exist you will need to help pay for it. Giving money allows you to express your desire and commitment to be part of a faith community and allows your commitment to be realized. All organizations should institute the diversity of fundraising methods that characterizes most religious institutions. In the chapters that follow, I will show you how.

2

Principles of Fundraising

Let's start with a question: "What is the purpose of fundraising?" Here is the wrong answer: "To raise money." The only way you can raise money year after year is by developing a broad base of individual donors who feel loyal to your organization. The purpose of fundraising, then, is to build those relationships, or more simply put, the purpose of fundraising is not to raise money, but to raise donors. You don't want gifts, you want givers. You want people to make donations and feel so good about how they were treated and what you did with the money that they want to give again and again. They may even tell their friends about your organization, so you not only get money from them but from new donors as well. Focusing on building a donor base rather than on simply raising money means that sometimes you will undertake a fundraising strategy that does not raise money in the first year, such as direct mail, or for several years, such as legacy giving. It means that you will relate to your donors as individual human beings rather than as ATMs that you engage when you want money but whom you otherwise ignore. It means you will plan for both the short term and the long term and look at the results of any fundraising strategy not only for the next month but also for the next few years. DIVERSIFYING SOURCES Focusing on raising donors means that an organization systematically diversifies its sources of funding, increases the number of people helping raise money, and diversifies the skills of those doing fundraising. The need for diversity is not a new lesson. People with only one skill have a more difficult time finding employment than those with a variety of skills. Investors put their money in a variety of financial instruments rather than in just one kind of stock. Since the 1980s thousands of nonprofits have been forced to curtail their services severely or to close their doors because the government funding they relied on so heavily ceased to be available. Yet many organizations continue to look for the ideal special event that will fund their entire budget, or they search for one person, foundation, or corporation who will give most of the money they need, or they try to hire the perfect fundraiser who will bring in all their income without anyone's help. These groups reason that if they could use one fundraising strategy that was absolutely certain, tried and true, their money worries would be over. Unfortunately, no fundraising strategy or person fits that description. In fact, only if it maintains a diversity of sources will an organization survive for the long term. What's the largest percentage of their income that an organization should rely on from one source? Think of it this way: an organization could lose 30 percent of its funding and probably survive, though it would be difficult, but the loss of more than 30 percent of funding would be catastrophic for all but the biggest organizations. That's why organizations should not receive more than 30 percent of their funding from any one source for more than one or two years. This guideline means that although you could have more than 30 percent of income coming from membership (and many groups do), you cannot have one member providing 30 percent of this money. (The IRS recognizes this principle with its "one-third rule," which states that an organization with one-third or more of its total income from one person, foundation, or corporation for more than three years does not meet the test of a public charity; if this condition persists for several years, an organization risks losing its 501(c)(3) status. Public charities are to be supported by a cross section of the public.) There is no set number of sources that constitutes healthy diversity. Much will depend on the size of your budget, your location, and your work. However, the more people who give you money and the more ways you have of raising money, the better off you are. WHY PEOPLE GIVE Approximately seven out of ten adults regularly make donations to nonprofits. Of those, most support between five and eleven organizations, giving away a little more than 2 percent of their personal income. All fundraising efforts should go toward trying to become one of the groups that these givers give to, rather than trying to become the recipient of the first charitable donation of a previous nongiver. People who give money are not denying themselves food or withholding shoes for their children; these people are dedicated givers, and your organization's job is to become one of those they give to. To do that you must carefully examine what makes a person a giver. Self-Interest There are many reasons that people give to nonprofit organizations. The most common reasons vary from consumerism to tradition to deeply held belief. Some people give because they like the newsletter an organization provides or because they receive a free tote bag, bumper sticker, or some other tangible item. Some give to a certain group because everyone in their social circle gives to that group or because it is a family tradition. Some give because it is the only way to get something the organization offers (classes, theater seats, access to a swimming pool). At a more altruistic level, there are more reasons for giving. People give because they care about the issue, they believe in the group, and they think the group's analysis of a problem and vision of a solution are correct. Often people give because they or someone they know were once in the position of the people the group serves (alcoholics, abused women or children, unemployed, homeless) or because they are thankful that neither they nor anyone they know is in that position. People give because the group expresses their own ideals and enables them to reinforce their image of themselves as a principled person—for example, a feminist, environmentalist, pacifist, equal rights advocate, good parent, concerned citizen, or whatever image is important to them. Through their giving, they can say in truth, "I am a caring person," "I have deep feelings for others," "I am helping others." Sometimes people give because they feel guilty about how much they have or what they have done in their own life, or they give in order to feel more assured of salvation and eternal life. Above all, however, people give because they are asked, and being asked reminds them what they care about. When they are asked personally by a friend or someone they admire, in addition to feeling good about giving to the organization, they get to show themselves as a principled and generous person to someone whose opinion they value. Although these motivations for giving are what impel most people to give, most nonprofit organizations appeal to two other potential motives that are not very persuasive. These are, "We need the money," and "Your gift is tax deductible."

Neither of these reasons distinguishes your organization from all the others. All nonprofit organizations claim to need money, and most of them do. The fact that the gift is tax deductible is a nice touch, but gifts to several hundred thousand other nonprofits are tax deductible too. Further, as I mentioned in Chapter One, the majority of Americans file a short form (that is, they do not itemize deductions to charities on their income tax returns), so they receive no tax benefits for their giving. Neither need nor tax advantage makes your organization special. Giving as Fee for Service The 70 percent of Americans who give away money pay nonprofits to do work that can only be accomplished by group effort. There is very little one person can do about racism or pollution or world hunger. Only as part of an organization can an individual make a difference in these or any other pressing social problems. Certainly, one person cannot be a theater or a museum or an alternative school. Donors need the organization as much as the organization needs them, and the money is given in exchange for work performed. In a way, donations are really fees for service. ANYONE CAN DO

FUNDRAISING Most important for small organizations, it is critical to understand that fundraising is easy to learn. In the past thirty years there has been an increasing emphasis on fundraising as a "discipline." Colleges and universities now offer courses on various aspects of fundraising, sometimes as part of degree programs in nonprofit management, and professional organizations offer certification programs in fundraising. There are more and more people who are professional fundraisers. All of these developments contribute to the health and well-being of the nonprofit sector. But a course, a degree, or certification is not required for a person to be good at fundraising, and they will never take the place of the only three things you really need in order to be a fundraiser: simple common sense, a commitment to a cause, and a basic affection for people. No one says at the age of twelve, "When I grow up, I want to be in fundraising." Instead, a person is drawn to an idea or cause and to an organization working on that issue. The organization needs money in order to pursue the cause, so the person decides to help with fundraising, even though it is not their first choice of how to be involved and even though they have at first found the idea of raising money slightly distasteful or a little frightening. With time and experience, many people find that fundraising is not as difficult as they had imagined; they may even begin to like it. They realize that people feel good about themselves when they give money to a cause they believe in and that to ask someone for money actually means to give that person an opportunity to express traditions or beliefs that are important to them. People asked to raise money often confuse the process of giving money and the process of asking for it. In fact, there is a significant difference between the two. People feel good about giving money, but rarely do people feel good when they ask for money until they get used to it. People asking for money for their cause tend to project their own feelings of discomfort in asking onto the potential donor and then describe the donor in words such as these: "I really embarrassed that person when I asked him," or "I could tell she wanted to leave the room when I asked her," or "They were so upset that they just looked at each other and finally said yes but I know they wanted to say no." These descriptions of how the donor supposedly felt (embarrassed, humiliated, upset) are more likely to be descriptions of how the asker was feeling. The potential donor was more than likely flattered, pleased to be included, thinking about what amount he or she could give, or wondering if the asker was feeling all right. The feelings of discomfort in asking for money are normal, and in Chapter Six I talk about them and how to deal with them. For now, be clear that asking and giving are two very different experiences, even when they happen in the same conversation. When people are recruited to ask for money, they must reflect on what they like about giving, not on what they hate about asking. When an organization has a diversity of ways to raise money, it can use the talents and abilities of all the people in the group to help with fundraising. As volunteers and board members learn more about fundraising and experience success doing it, they will be willing to learn new strategies and they will begin to like asking for money. Further, an organization that has only one or two people raising its money is not much better off than an organization that has only one or two sources of money. Many small organizations have suffered more from having too few people doing the fundraising than from having too few sources of funds. In the chapters that follow, I discuss how to identify appropriate fundraising strategies and how to build a team of volunteer fundraisers.

3

Fundraising Strategies with Financial Needs

Organizations have three financial needs: the money they need to operate every year, not surprisingly called annual needs; the money they need to improve their building or upgrade their capacity to do their work, called capital needs; and a permanent income stream to ensure financial stability and assist long-term planning, the source of which is either an endowment or a reserve fund. ANNUAL NEEDS Most organizations spend most of their time raising money for the program needs of the current year. This kind of fundraising is often referred to as the "annual fund" or the "annual drive," or to cover all tracks, the "annual fund drive." The annual fund uses several strategies, such as Internet, direct mail, special events, phoning, and personal visits. The purpose of the annual fund is to acquire new donors and to get current donors to give again and if possible, to give bigger gifts. Because the overall purpose of fundraising is to build a base of donors who give you money every year, it is helpful to analyze how a person becomes a donor to an organization and how, ideally, that person increases their loyalty to the group and expresses that increased loyalty with a steady increase in giving. In moving from having never given to a particular group to giving regularly year after year and sometimes several times a year, a person goes through three phases. The first phase starts when a person is asked to give to an organization she hears or reads about and likes the sound of and decides on the spur of the moment to make a donation. That first gift is called an "impulse" gift. Even if an impulse gift is fairly large, it will rarely reflect what the donor could really afford and it is generally based on little knowledge or commitment to the organization. This is the moment at which the organization seeks to move this donor to the second phase. The donor is thanked as soon as possible, then several times during the course of the year the donor is asked for additional gifts to different aspects of the organization's work. Ideally, the donor is asked in a few different ways, such as by phone, at an event, or with a personal letter. If the donor continues to give for three or more years, she is called a "habitual" donor. Habitual donors see themselves as part of the organization and identify with the work and the victories of the organization. Some habitual donors have a bigger commitment to the organization than their gift reflects and have the capacity to make a bigger gift. Identifying and asking these people to increase their gift forms the basis of a major donor program. Once donors are giving larger gifts than they give to most other groups, they have entered the third phase, called "thoughtful" giving. Instead of just giving what they are in the habit of giving, they now think about what they can afford and how making a large gift to one group will affect their other giving. The process of moving people from nondonor to donor, then to habitual donor and from there to thoughtful donor is the main focus in planning the annual fund. To maintain its annual income, an organization has to recruit a certain number of new donors every year, upgrade a certain number of regular donors into major donors, and give all their donors three or four chances to give extra gifts. A note on asking several times a year: Some people say they dislike receiving several appeals a year from a group. But because one donor doesn't like to be asked more than once a year, it doesn't mean that most people are like that. Many people don't even notice how often they are asked, particularly if you are using a few different strategies. Some donors give every time they are asked, and many donors find being asked a few times a year a good way to keep up with the work of the organization. However, since fundraising is a process of building relationships, if a donor says to you, "I only give once a year, so please only ask me once a year," then you will go into your database and suppress their name for any extra appeals. If a donor says, "Don't ever call me on the phone," you similarly note in their file not to call that person. An organization can expect to retain about two-thirds of its individual donors every year, with the greatest proportion of their one-third loss being people who give once and not again. In planning fundraising strategies, then, you need to have a few strategies for the sole purpose of replacing lost donors. Organizations that lose a lot fewer than one-third of their donor base most likely do not have enough donors—almost any group can keep a small group of donors renewing year in and year out. You want to grow big enough that you are bringing in a lot of new donors, knowing that up to one-third of them will not stay. Organizations that lose more than one-third of their donors are not doing enough to keep them, and in the case of most grassroots organizations, this situation usually means they are not asking donors for money often enough. Remember, every organization the donor belongs to is asking several times a year, and the donor is also being solicited by other groups. If you only ask once a year, you become an minuscule percentage of the solicitations the donor receives. In fact, many lapsed donors will report that they never remember receiving any requests from the group and that it was not their intent for their membership to lapse. To retain your donors, you need to have a few strategies designed just for them. Section Two discusses these strategies in more detail. Finally, you need to have some strategies to get current donors to give more money—these are called upgrading strategies. Sections Two and Three discuss a wide variety of these strategies and their uses.

An organization has three goals for every donor. The first is for that person to get to the point of being a thoughtful donor—to give the biggest gift he or she can afford on a yearly basis. (Such a gift usually comes from the donor's annual income.) The second goal is for as many donors as possible to give gifts to a capital or other special campaign. These do not have to be connected to capital improvements, but they are gifts that are unusual in some way and are only given a few times, or possibly only once, during the donor's lifetime. Capital gifts are usually given from the donors' assets, such as savings, inheritance, or property. A donor cannot afford to give assets every year, so will only give such a gift for a special purpose. The third goal is for every donor to remember the organization in their will or to make some kind of arrangement benefiting the organization from their estate. An estate gift is arranged during the donor's lifetime but wholly received by the organization on the donor's death. Obviously, these gifts are made only once. Most small organizations will do well if they can plan a broad range of strategies to acquire, maintain, and upgrade annual gifts, but over time organizations need to think about capital and endowment gifts and learn to use fundraising strategies that will encourage such gifts. Grassroots organizations do receive bequests and gifts of property, art, appreciated stock, and the like. Only by asking will you find out what your donors might be willing and able to do for your group.

Because all strategies are directed toward building relationships with funding sources—whether these sources are individuals, as this book stresses, or foundations, corporations, or government—it is important to understand the types of strategies that create or improve relationships with donors. There are three broad categories of strategies—acquisition, retention, and upgrade—and they directly relate to the cycles that donors follow: giving impulsively, giving habitually, and giving thoughtfully. Acquisition Strategies. The main purpose of these strategies is to get people who have not given to your group before to give for the first time. Direct mail appeals, Web site asks, or certain special events are the most common acquisition strategies. Acquisition strategies seek impulse donors, and the income from them is generally used for the organization's annual fund. Retention Strategies. These strategies seek to get donors to give a second time, a third time, and so on, until they are donors of habit. The income from retention strategies is also used for annual needs. Upgrading Strategies. These strategies aim to get donors to give more than they have given previously—to give a bigger gift regularly and later to give gifts of assets and a gift of their estate. Upgrading is done almost entirely through personal solicitation, although it can be augmented by mail or phone contact or through certain special events. Upgrading strategies seek to move habitual donors to being thoughtful donors. The income from thoughtful donors is used for annual, capital, and endowment needs, depending on the nature of the gift or the campaign for which the gift was sought.

As you create a fundraising plan, note beside each strategy you intend to use whether you are using it for acquiring, retaining, or upgrading donors, and make sure it is the best strategy for that purpose.

For small organizations, the ultimate reason to be thoughtful about fundraising strategies is to work smarter, not harder. The group in the house party example raised 400 percent more money in their second year of house parties by spending a little more time to think about the strategy more thoroughly. Small organizations with tight budgets have little room for errors that result from carelessness and lack of thought. It is clear to me from years of working with nonprofit organizations that you can never save time. You can put time in on the front end, planning, thinking things through, and doing things right, or you can "save time" on the front end only to have to put it in later clearing up the mess, handling disgruntled donors, and having to do more fundraising because what you have done did not raise the money you need. This book will help you be a front-end time user!

4
Asking for Money

In studies in which people are asked why they gave the last donation they made, about 80 percent say, "Because someone asked me." Of course, millions of smaller fundraising requests are done in person—canvassing, Girl Scout cookie sales, raffle ticket sales, Salvation Army buckets, panhandling, and so on all have a strong element of personal asking. These forms of personal solicitation will not have the 50 percent rate of success unless the solicitor is known to each potential donor, but they will have a higher rate of success than methods that don't use a face-to-face approach. Strategies to raise more substantial gifts for nonprofits, including major gifts programs, capital campaigns, and endowment drives, rely for success on personal solicitation. Despite these facts, personal solicitation is one of the most difficult strategies to implement. It requires that people engage in an activity—asking for money— that most of us have been taught is rude or just not done. However, for organizations that are serious about fundraising, and particularly for organizations that would like to increase the number of people in their donor base who give at least $500 annually, learning how to ask for money in person is imperative. WHY WE'RE AFRAID TO ASK FOR MONEY If the idea of asking for money fills you with anxiety, disgust, dread, or some combination of these feelings, you are among the majority of people. If asking for money does not cause you any distress, you have either let go of your fear about it, you grew up in an household of unusually liberated attitudes toward money, or you may have come from a country that does not consider talking about money as taboo. To identify the sources of our fears, we must look at both the role of money in American society and the attitudes about asking for anything that are the legacy of the strong Puritan ethic that is our American heritage. Most of us were taught that money, sex, religion, death, and politics are all taboo topics for discussion with anyone other than perhaps one's most intimate friends or *family. Mental illness, age, race, and related topics are often added to this list of inappropriate topics. Discomfort in talking about any of them will be stronger in some parts of the country or among some generations. The taboo on talking about money, however, is far stronger than any of the others. Many of us were taught to believe that inquiring about a person's salary or asking how much he or she paid for a house or a car is rude. Even today it is not unusual for one spouse not to know how much the other spouse earns, for children not to know how much their parents earn, or for close friends not to know each other's income. Further, few people really understand how the economy works. They don't know the meaning of things they hear and read about every day—the stock market, for example, including the difference between a bear and a bull market, or what the rising or falling of the various stock market indices mean. In the past thirty years, more and more social justice groups have recognized that economic literacy is a key component in community organizing, but it will take decades to reverse the general ignorance about how the economy works and more important, how it could work. Many people, misquoting the Christian New Testament, say, "Money is the root of all evil." In fact, Paul's letter to Timothy says, "For the love of money is the root of all evil. Some people, in their passion for it, have strayed from the faith and have come to grief amid great pain." In truth, money in itself has no good or evil qualities. It is a substance made of paper or metal. It has no constant value, and it has no morality. It can be used well or badly. It can buy guns or flowers. Good people need it just as much as evil ones. It is simply a means of exchange. People will also say, "Money doesn't buy happiness" as a way of minimizing the power of money; they often go on to describe unhappy rich people they have known or read about, though most people secretly think that they would be happier if they had more money. Our attitudes about money are changing, giving us more mixed messages than ever. For example, in the 1990s many young people in the computer industry felt they were failures if they hadn't made a million dollars by the time they were thirty. (I'm often amazed at the lack of perspective in this aspiration: most people have no idea what percentage of the world's population lives in poverty or how many children starve to death every day.) More recently, a general rule widely publicized is that one must have at least a million dollars saved in order to retire with any degree of comfort, even though reaching that sum is completely unrealistic for most American workers. In another example of financial blindness, large corporations are often considered successful despite operating at a loss and are simply kept afloat by investor optimism. Sadly, our attitudes toward money change but do not get healthier. Money is shrouded in mystery and tinged with fascination. Most people are curious about the salary levels of their friends, how much money their neighbors have inherited, how the super-rich live. How much money you have and how long you have had it denotes class distinctions and helps each of us place ourselves in relation to others—even while we maintain the myth that our country is a classless meritocracy. Consequently, people speculate a great deal about the place of money in others' lives. Money is like sex and sexuality in this regard: kept in secrecy and therefore alluring. But just as much of what we learned as children and teenagers about sex turned out to be untrue, so it is with money. The comedian Kate Clinton says she was raised to think about sex like this: "Sex is dirty. Save it for someone you love." Most of us can relate to that and can see much of what we learned about money in that same light: "Money is evil. Get a lot of it." One major effect of money being a taboo topic is that only those willing to learn about it can control it. In the United States, an elite and fairly secret class controls most of the nation's wealth, either by earning it, having inherited it, or both. It serves the interest of this ruling class for the rest of us not to know who controls money and how to gain control of it ourselves. As long as we cannot ask about other people's salaries, we will not be able to find out that someone is being paid more because he is white or less because she is a woman. As long as we do not understand basic economics, we will not be able to advocate for or even know what the most progressive tax structure is, finance our nonprofits adequately, or create a society in which wealth is more fairly and equally distributed, which is, after all, the main underlying goal of social justice movements. Political activists and participants in social change must learn how to raise money effectively and ethically, how to manage it carefully, and how to spend it wisely. In fact, activists who refuse to learn about money, including how to ask for it, wind up collaborating with the very system that the rest of their work is designed to change. The idea of asking for money raises another set of hindering attitudes, which are largely the inheritance of a predominately Protestant culture infused with a Puritan ethic that affects most Americans, including those who are not Protestants. This set of values conveys a number of messages that influence our feelings and actions. For example, a Puritan ethic implies that if you are a good person and you work hard you will get what you deserve. It further implies that if you have to ask for something you are a weak person, because strong people are self-sufficient. Further, the mythology continues, if you have to ask for help, most likely you have not worked hard enough and you probably don't deserve it. Rounding out this series of beliefs is our deep distrust in the ability of government to solve social problems and a general conviction that the government wastes our money. All of these beliefs can be found among people on both the left and the right sides of the political spectrum as well as across age and race lines and all religious orientations. Where these beliefs will not be found is in two places: Other countries. Although many countries have various taboos related to money, none have as many self-canceling and contradictory ones as the United States. Our taboos about money are not universal.*

Children. Children have no trouble asking for money. They do not subscribe to the idea that self-sufficiency means not asking or that polite people don't ask. They ask, and they ask again and again. Our taboos about money are not natural—we are not born with them. Our beliefs about money are learned, and therefore they can be unlearned. The wonderful writer Ursula LeGuin once said in a lecture, "I never learned much from my teachers, but I learned a great deal from my un-teachers: the people who said to me, 'You shouldn't have learned that and you don't need to think it anymore.'" Fundraising for social change is in part about raising the money we need, but over a longer period of time it is also about creating healthy attitudes toward money, and many people find that aspect of fundraising to be most fascinating. To get over your own anxieties about money, it is helpful to reflect on how you were raised to think about money and about how you want to relate to money now that you are an adult. It takes time and work, but you can adopt new and healthier attitudes toward money. SPECIFIC FEARS With these very strong taboos operating against asking for money, it is a wonder that anyone ever does it! Understanding the source of our discomfort is the first step toward overcoming it. The next step is to examine our fears of what will happen to us when we do ask for money. When people look at their fears rationally they often find that most of them disappear or at least become manageable. Fears about asking for money fall into three categories: · Those that will almost never happen ("The person will hit me." "I'll die of a heart attack during the solicitation.") · Those that could be avoided with training and preparation ("I won't know what to say.""I won't know my facts, the person will think I am an idiot.") · Those that definitely will happen sometimes, maybe as much as half the time ("The person will say no.") In the last category—things that will happen—most people not only fear the possible outcome that the person will say no; many also fear that asking will have a negative effect on a friendship and that a gift from a friend will obligate them to give to the friend's cause in turn. Let's look at each of these more closely.

"The Person Will Say No." Rejection is the number-one fear. Unfortunately, being told no will happen at least as often as being told yes. Therefore, it is important to get to the point where you don't feel upset when someone says no. You do this by realizing that when you ask someone for a gift, you are seeing

them at a single moment in their lives. A thousand things have happened to the person prior to your request, none of which has anything to do with you but many of which will affect the person's receptiveness to your request. For example, the person may have recently found out that one of their children needs braces, that their car needs new tires, or that a client is not able to pay a bill on time. This news may affect the prospect's perception of what size donation he or she can make. The person may wish your organization success but may have already given away all the money they can at this time or may have determined other priorities for their giving this year. Events unrelated to money can also cause the prospect to say no: a divorce proceeding, a death in the family, a headache. As the solicitor, none of these things is your fault. Many of them you could not have known ahead of time and you may never learn them because the prospect keeps them private. By feeling personally rejected you misinterpret the prospect's response and flatter yourself that you had something to do with it. As the asker, you have to remember that, above all, the person being asked has the right to say no to a request without offering a reason. Most of the time you will not know exactly why your request was turned down. Your job is not to worry about why this prospect said no but to go on, undaunted, to the next prospect. "Asking a Friend for Money Will Have a Negative Effect on Our Friendship." Many people feel that friendship is outside the realm of money. They feel that to bring money into a friendship is to complicate it and perhaps to ruin it. Friends are usually the best prospects, however, because they share our commitments and values. They are interested in our lives and wish us success and happiness. To many people's surprise, friends are more likely to be offended or hurt when they are not asked. They can't understand why you don't want to include them in your work. Further, if it is truly acceptable to you for a person to say no to your request, your friend will never feel put on the spot. Your friend will not feel pressured by your request, as if your whole friendship hung on the answer. When asking friends, make clear that yes is the answer you are hoping for, but no is also acceptable. Say something like, "I don't know what your other commitments are, but I wanted to invite you to be part of this if you can." "If the Person Says Yes to My Request I Will Be Obligated to Give to Their Cause Whether I Want to or Not." This quid pro quo situation ("this for that") does happen from time to time, and it happens frequently with some people. Giving money to a cause at the request of a friend so that you can ask them later for your own cause, or feeling you must give because your friend gave to your cause is not fundraising. It is simply trading money; it would be cheaper and easier to just give to your cause and let your friend give to theirs. Also, a person who gives out of obligation to a friend will not become a habitual donor. They will cease to give as soon as their friend is no longer involved. If someone you ask for money gives to your organization, you are not obligated to that person except to make sure that the organization uses the money wisely and for the purpose you solicited. The obligation is fulfilled if the organization is honest and does its work. The solicitor does not materially benefit from a solicitation. They present the cause and if the prospect is sympathetic, he or she agrees to help support it. The cause was furthered. Beyond a thank you note and a gracious attitude, the solicitor owes the donor nothing. If the donor then asks you to support his or her cause, you consider the request without reference to your previous request or its result. You may wish to support the person or the cause, but you are not obligated to do so. If you think that someone is going to attach strings to a gift, don't ask that prospect. There are hundreds of prospects who will give freely. Far from being a horrible thing to do, asking someone for money actually does them a favor. People who agree with your goals and respect the work of your group will want to be a part of it. Giving money is a simple and effective way to be involved, to be part of a cause larger than oneself. Many volunteers find that it takes practice to overcome their fears about asking for money. To begin soliciting donations does not require being free of fear; it only requires having your fear under control. Ask yourself if what you believe in is bigger than what you are afraid of. An old fundraising saying is that if you are afraid to ask someone for a gift, "Kick yourself out of the way and let your cause do the talking." The point is this: if you are committed to an organization, you will do what is required to keep that organization going, which includes asking for money.

5

Special Events

Special events, also often called "fundraising benefits," are social gatherings of many sorts that expand the reputation of the organization; give those attending an amusing, interesting, or moving time; and possibly make money for the organization sponsoring the event. The variety of special events is practically limitless, as are the possibilities for money earned or lost, amount of work put in, number of people participating, and so on. Special events are arguably the oldest fundraising strategy and certainly the most common around the world. In every country where I have taught fundraising or read about fundraising, special events have played a big role. Because of their variety and flexibility, special events are excellent strategies for acquiring, retaining, or upgrading donors, and organizations that are serious about building a broad base of individual donors need to have at least one or two special events every year. Events are often misunderstood and misused. What they do well—increase visibility—is often not the goal, and what they do badly—raise lots of money—is too often the only thing people are seeking when they plan them. Keep in mind, then, that special events should have three goals: · To generate publicity for the organization · To raise the visibility of the organization · To bring in (new) money Generating Publicity. Generating publicity means getting a particular audience to pay attention to the organization for a limited time by means of advertising the event and by the quality of the event itself.Enhancing Visibility. An event raises the overall profile of the organization in the community. Visibility is the cumulative effect of publicity. With each successive event, and in combination with other fundraising and organizing efforts, the organization becomes known to more and more of the people who should know about it. The visibility of your group can be assessed by asking this question: Of the people who should know about you, what percentage do? This percentage is called your visibility quotient. Assessing a visibility *quotient requires thinking through what types of people should know about your organization and what mechanisms reach those potential donors. For example, if you are regularly featured in the local newspaper, you may be well known to those who read the paper, but you also need to reach people who don't read any newspapers, which is now a majority of young people and larger and larger numbers of all people. In that case, getting more print publicity will not help you; you may need to move to radio, speaking engagements at houses of worship, or a door-to-door canvass in order to reach new constituencies. Events are excellent publicity-generating tools because they give the media a hook around which to focus attention on the group. A newspaper or radio station may be interested in discussing the event or even doing a profile of it—an auction, self-defense class, or concert—and will mention the sponsoring group's name, thus raising visibility. Raising Money. Raising money is a secondary goal for a special event because there are many faster and easier ways to raise money than this one. An organization that simply needs money (perhaps from being in a cash flow bind or having an unexpected expense) will find that the slowest ways to raise that money are seeking government funding or having an event. On the other hand, an organization that wants to raise its profile, bring in new people, and possibly make money will find a special event an ideal strategy. In many cases special events can lose money or barely break even and still be successful because of the publicity and visibility they produced. TYPES OF PEOPLE WHO ATTEND SPECIAL EVENTS There are two categories of people who attend events: those who come because of the event itself and those who come both for the event and to support your group. In the first category are people who would come to a particular event no matter who sponsored it. These people attend flea markets, dances, movie benefits, decorator showcases, auctions, and the like. Many times these people will not even know the name of the group sponsoring the event. In a similar vein are small businesses or corporations that will buy ads in an adbook, donate raffle prizes, buy tables at luncheons, or even underwrite an event but would not give an organization money under other circumstances. They want the advertising and resulting goodwill the event gives them, along with the chance to target a specific audience inexpensively. Raising money from a person or a business that would not give you money otherwise does not constitute donor "acquisition," but it is a smart use of an event and provides another income stream. Of course, the event should also be designed to draw people who are interested in your group. However, for organizations in rural communities or serving a very small constituency and unable to build a large base of donors, events that draw people to the event rather than the cause will be important for* *raising money. The second type of people who attend events are those who are both interested in the event and believe in your group's work. They may not have heard of your organization before learning of this event, or they may already know of your organization and want to support it while getting something important to them. For example, women wanting to take a self-defense class may choose one sponsored by the local rape crisis program rather than a commercial gym in order to support the rape crisis program. After the classes, some of the participants may want to join the program as volunteers and paying members. People who buy all their holiday presents at a crafts fair put on by a public radio station or who enter marathons sponsored by groups they believe in are good prospects to follow up with direct mail or e-mail appeals. Among the second type are people who appreciate your organization's work but can't afford or don't want to donate more than a small sum. For them, buying a $1 raffle ticket or attending a $6 movie benefit is a perfect way to show their support. CHOOSING A FUNDRAISING EVENT Several criteria should be considered in choosing a fundraising event: the appropriateness of the event, the image of the organization created by the event, the amount of volunteer energy required, the amount of front money needed, the repeatability and the timing of the event, and how the event fits into the organization's overall fundraising plan.*

In addition to being appropriate, the event as much as possible should be in keeping with the image of the organization or should promote the image the organization wishes to have. Although considerations of appropriateness sometimes include those of image, image is also a distinct issue. Many events that are appropriate for a group do not promote a memorable image of it. For example, a library would choose a book sale over a garage sale, even though both are appropriate. An environmental organization would use a whitewater rafting trip over season tickets to the ballet as a door prize, even though both are nice prizes. An organization promoting awareness of the problem of high blood pressure might choose a health fair over a dance. The idea is to attract people to your event who might become regular donors to your organization by linking the event to your mission. Energy of Volunteers Looking at the volunteer energy required to plan and mount an event involves several considerations. How many people are required to put on this event? What would these volunteers be doing if they were not working on this event? Do you have enough volunteers who have the time required to produce this event—not only to manage the event on the day of its occurrence but to take care of all the details that must be done beforehand? Volunteer time is a resource to be cultivated, guided, and used appropriately. For example, don't use someone with connections to major donor prospects to sell T-shirts at a shopping mall on Saturday afternoon. Similarly, a friendly, outgoing person who loves to talk on the phone should be the phone-a-thon coordinator or the solicitor of auction items and not be asked to bake brownies for the food booth at the county fair. Obviously, what the volunteer wants to do should be of primary concern. People generally like to do what they are good at and be involved where they can be most useful. Front Money Most special events require that some money be spent before there is assurance that any money will be raised. The front money needed for an event should be an amount your organization could afford to lose if the event had to be canceled. This money should already be available—you should not, for example, use funds from advance ticket sales to rent the place where the event will be held. If the event is canceled some people will want their money back, but you may not get your whole rent deposit back. Events that require a lot of front money can create a cash flow problem in the organization if the need for this money is not taken into account. Repeatability The best event is one that becomes a tradition in your community, so that every year people look forward to the event that your group sponsors. Using this criterion can save you from discarding an event simply because the turnout was small the first time you did it. Perhaps you got too little publicity and only a handful of people came. If each of those people had a great time and you heard them saying, "I wish I had brought Juan," or "I wish Tiffany had known about this," then it may be worth having the event again next year. To decide if an event is repeatable, evaluate whether the same number of people working the same number of hours would raise more money producing this event again. Timing You need to find out what else is happening in your community at the time you want to hold your event. You don't want to conflict with the major fundraising event of a similar organization, nor do you want to be the tenth dance or auction in a row. If you are appealing to a particular constituency, you need to think of their timing. Farmers are mostly unavailable during planting and harvest seasons; Jews will not appreciate being invited to a buffet on Yom Kippur; gay men and lesbians may not come to a silent meditation scheduled during the Gay and Lesbian Pride Parade, and so on. The Big Picture The final consideration is the place of the event in the overall fundraising picture. If you find that the same people attend all your organization's events as well as give money by mail, you are "eating your own tail" and need to rethink how you are using events. If you cannot seem to get publicity for your events or you are unable to find an event to reach new constituencies, then maybe special events is not the right approach. If after analyzing your donor base you decide that your organization needs to increase its number of thoughtful donors, then you won't do as many events whose main purpose is acquisition. In other words, the results of special events (new names, publicity, new volunteers) must be fed into the overall effort to build a donor base or the effort of the event will have mostly been wasted.

HOW TO PLAN A SPECIAL EVENT Special events require more planning time than one would imagine. Because so much can go wrong, and because many things often hinge on one thing so that one mistake can throw off weeks of work, events must be planned with more attention to minute detail than almost any other fundraising strategy. The Committee for Special Events There must be a small committee of volunteers overseeing the work for the event. If an event is so complicated that it is unrealistic for volunteers to be able to manage (a conference, a giant gala, a multiday fair), then hire an event planner. Using your own paid staff to plan and carry out a special event is not a good use of their time. Presumably, this is not what they were hired to do, it is not their expertise, and if you factor in the cost of their time on the event and the opportunity cost of what they are not doing while they are working on the event, you will see that your event is costing a much larger amount of money than the budget for it indicates. The job of the committee is to plan and coordinate the event, not to do every task. After planning the event, most of the committee's work is delegating as many tasks as possible. Keep the committee to between five and seven people. Larger committees are unwieldy and can be counterproductive. With a larger committee planning the event, it is likely that the planning process will take longer, that the committee meetings will be like special events themselves, and the committee members will burn out and not want to help with this or any other event again. It is also likely that a large committee will have only five real workers. Each special event should have its own committee, although there can be overlap from one event to another. Special events are labor intensive, however, and people need to have a rest period between events and a chance not to participate in every one. The committee must have staff and board support, and everyone must agree that the chosen event is a good idea. Tasks of the Committee There are three simple steps a special events committee should take to ensure the success of the event: detail a master task list, prepare a budget, and create a timeline.

6
Using Mail

Direct mail is a strategy of sending a form letter that asks for money to hundreds, thousands, or even millions of people by bulk mail. It is a strategy widely used in the United States, Canada, Australia, and England, but not used at all in countries where people don't send money (in the form of checks, money orders, or credit card authorizations) through the mail. Direct mail is greatly augmented by the Internet; in some places and with some causes online giving has overtaken using postal mail in popularity. You may be tempted to skip this chapter if you think that your organization will focus on raising money through the Internet or other strategies; however, the psychology of direct mail is important to understand and is useful in almost any communication you have with donors. Further, direct mail remains the only strategy that allows you to get something tangible (an envelope containing a request) into the hands of anyone served by the U.S. Postal Service for about $1 per address. Used carefully, the return is not only gaining numbers of new donors and eventually a solid income stream, but identifying donors to whom you had no other access. Stories abound of donors recruited through direct mail whom no one in the organization had ever met sending $500 and $1,000 in response to a first appeal, or donors whom no one knew leaving an organization money through a bequest after giving $35 a year for years and years. I emphasize throughout this book that all strategies must be used in conjunction with each other. Direct mail, as you will see, is the most obvious example of this tenet. A direct mail appeal is very simple: it contains a letter describing the organization and its needs and a self-addressed envelope, making it easy for the donor to return a gift. Even with the Internet, direct mail is still the most common fundraising strategy in use today. Letters that are addressed to an individual—"Dear Mrs. Smith"—or letters sent by first-class mail are not technically considered direct mail pieces, although these more *personalized letters may borrow from direct mail principles in their look or style of writing, and identical text may be going to dozens— or thousands—of recipients. In the United States, direct mail letters are sent in minimum quantities of two hundred, presorted by ZIP code for the post office; at the post office they receive bottom priority for processing in return for a deep discount in the postage. Direct mail solicitation (often derisively called "junk mail") has been in wide use since World War II. In the 1970s and 1980s, direct mail fundraising was so popular that many organizations derived the bulk of their income from it. Over time, as the market has become saturated with it, its effectiveness has decreased. People have become accustomed to receiving direct mail, making letters from groups one never heard of no longer as interesting to open. To get a sense of the volume of direct mail, consider that 40 percent of the total mail in the world is generated in the United States and that 40 percent of that mail is direct mail, both from commercial and nonprofit sources. This means that about one out of every six pieces of mail worldwide is direct mail. For many Americans, far more than one out of six pieces coming through their mail slots is an unsolicited fundraising letter. Some fundraising professionals (and probably thousands of consumers) have questioned whether direct mail continues to be an effective fundraising strategy. Despite all the bad publicity it gets, however, direct mail remains the least expensive way to reach the most people with a message that they can hold in their hands and examine at their leisure. A well-designed and well-written direct mail piece sent to a good list can still yield a response that makes it worthwhile: 0.75 to 1 percent on a first-time response, and 10 percent and often more from donors who have given before. Many groups also use direct mail letters to communicate with current donors and to ask for additional gifts. Used properly, direct mail is one of the most powerful strategies a small nonprofit can have. I am going to describe how direct mail works in a larger organization and then how a grassroots organization can adapt it to their circumstances.*

THREE FUNCTIONS OF DIRECT MAIL Direct mail soliciting has three functions; along with special events, it is one of the most versatile methods for developing closer relationships with donors. The three functions overlap with the strategies discussed in Chapter Three: acquisition, retention, and upgrading of donors. Get Someone to Give for the First Time. Donor acquisition is the main reason many organizations use direct mail. To see how it works, consider the experience of People for Good. People for Good trades five thousand names of their donors for an equal number of names of donors to another group, Friends of Progress. People for Good compares the names they got from Friends of Progress with their own donor list and pulls out anyone who already gives to both groups.*

To the rest of Friends of Progress, People for Good sends a direct mail appeal asking for a donation to their work. They get a 1 percent response, which is fifty gifts. Their cost was $1 for each piece of mail (including postage, printing, paper, and the use of a mail house), for a total cost of $5,000. Most of the fifty donors give $40, which is the suggested donation, but three give $25, ten give $50, three give $100, one gives $250, and one gives $500. They also experience an increase in traffic to their Web site and a few donations are made online, but they can't attribute that directly to this appeal, so they don't count it in their analysis. (It is common in fundraising to report the "average" gift, but this number can be misleading. In this example, the average gift was $58 because a few bigger gifts came in. Use "mode"—the gift received most often—and "median"—the midpoint, at which there is the same number of gifts above this point as below it—for meaningful analysis. In this example, knowing that most people gave the amount that was asked for—the mode gift—indicates that the amount suggested was reasonable.)

People for Good brings in $2,905 on the mailing, giving them a net cost of $2,095—that is, the income subtracted from their $5,000 cost, or about $42 for each of the fifty donors they acquired. These donors will now be moved to the next stage. From this accounting, you can see right from the start that there is no point in starting a direct mail program unless you are willing to go all the way with it, because the first mailing usually loses money and sometimes a lot of money. Read on to see how that money will not only be recouped, but grow. Get Donors to Repeat Their Gift. Once a person becomes a donor, the organization tries to get that person to give routinely. The best way to do that is to thank the donor within seventy-two hours of receiving their gift and then to ask the donors for money more than once a year. Small organizations should ask their current donors for money at least two or three times a year, either through the mail or with a combination of mail, phone solicitations, and special events. These requests are interspersed with newsletters (paper or e-newsletters or both). This frequency of asking will not offend people and keeps the name of your group in the donor's consciousness. It also enables you to take advantage of the ups and downs of each donor's cash flow situation. Every time you ask your donors for an extra gift by mail, you can expect that about 10 percent of them will respond. In this phase you make back the money you spent acquiring these people. Keep in mind that most people making a first gift will not make a second gift, but more people who make a second gift will make a third, and most people who make a third gift will make a fourth, and so on, assuming the organization continues to do good work and treats their donors properly. Get Donors to Renew Their Gift. To be considered active (as opposed to lapsed), donors must make a contribution at least once a *year, thus renewing their commitment to the organization. Most organizations have a renewal rate of about 66 percent—which is enough to generate a profit, including making back all the money you have invested in acquisition. Donors acquired through direct mail who show their commitment to the organization by renewing their gift are donors the organization might not have found otherwise who can be asked to volunteer, to give more money, to help with fundraising, to show up at demonstrations, and so on.*

USING DIRECT MAIL ON A SMALLER SCALE By now, you are probably thinking, "Well, that counts my group out. We don't have the money, we don't have the lists, and we can't wait a year or two for the repeat gifts and renewals to start making money." Don't despair. There is a way for even small groups to use mail appeals effectively. They must decrease the risk by decreasing the amount of money spent on each mailing. At the same time, they must try to increase the response rate so that they at least break even on first-time mailings to a list and with luck, make money. These goals can be achieved in two ways: by mailing to more carefully selected lists and by mailing to fewer people at one time. In the example above, we used the conventional estimate of a 1 percent response from a new list; this estimate is useful for planning costs. However, direct mail expert Mal Warwick cautions, "There is so much variation in response from one organization to another and from one appeal to another that using this 1 percent figure as success can steer organizations onto the wrong path." Factors such as attracting bigger donors, finding a whole new constituency of donors, testing messages, and so on are often as important as the percentage of response. Attracting a smaller response on the first mailing but a higher percentage of donors who renew year in and year out would make the mailing worth its costs. Despite this optimism, small organizations need some measurable gauge, and percentage of response will give you a way to budget money spent for money earned. Let's look at a direct mail scenario again but on a much smaller scale and with much more targeted lists.

DEVELOPING LISTS FOR MAIL APPEALS The cornerstone for the success of any mail appeal is the list of people who receive it. Compile or choose lists carefully. Make sure that each person's name is spelled correctly and that the address and ZIP code are correct. People tend to be miffed when their name is misspelled, and a wrong ZIP code will mean the letter won't be delivered. Lists are divided into three categories of expectation, which describe the likelihood of people on that list making a donation. These categories are hot, warm, and cold. Hot Lists. A hot list consists of people who have already made some kind of commitment to your organization. In order of decreasing heat, these people are your current donors, from whom can you expect a 10 percent response to any one mail appeal and of whom you can expect 66 percent to give a second time; lapsed donors from the past two years (expect a 3 to 7 percent response rate); volunteers and board members who are not yet donors (various response rates depending on the group; however, the response rate should not be lower than 5 percent and could be as high as 95 percent with good follow-up); and the close friends and associates of all of the above people who are not yet donors (2 to 5 percent response rate). Warm Lists. A warm list consists of people who have either used or heard of your services, people who are donors to organizations similar to yours but have not heard of your group, or people who have come to your special events. These lists should yield a 1 percent response rate but also give you donors you may not have other access to. Cold Lists. A cold list is any list that is more than a year old or any list of people about whom you know little or nothing. The phone book is an example of a cold list.

Some people will send only one or two names, and most people will not send any, but others will send in dozens of names. With a mailing list of one thousand donors, you can be assured of getting at least two hundred names from this type of appeal. Many organizations regularly remind their current donors to send in names of potential contributors by including a coupon in their newsletter and a request for names in other appeals. Another source of hot prospects is your board members, volunteers, and staff. On a yearly basis these people should also be asked to provide a list of names, which can be compared to the current mailing list; anyone who is not already a donor can be solicited. Of course, any board member, staff person, or volunteer who isn't already a donor is a hot prospect as well.

Some statisticians claim that every person knows 250 people—relatives, school friends, colleagues, neighbors, and so on. Of this number, perhaps only ten or twenty will be suitable prospects. Nevertheless, with each volunteer or member contributing some names, you will soon have the two hundred needed for a bulk mailing. For rural organizations or groups just starting out, don't wait until you have two hundred names—go ahead and send the letter by first-class mail. Warm Lists People who buy any of your organization's products, such as booklets, educational materials, and T-shirts, are excellent prospects for a mail appeal because they are known buyers. Certainly, their names should be kept so you can advertise any new items you produce to them, and some of them will become members of your organization. The same is true of people who attend conferences, seminars, or public meetings that you sponsor. To keep mailing costs down, you can also ask people who buy products or attend seminars you have sponsored for their e-mail address and advertise to them that way (see also Chapter Thirteen for more about enewsletters). People who attend special events who are not donors should receive an appeal soon after the event. Pass out a sign-up sheet or conduct a door prize drawing to get names and addresses. People who previously gave your organization money but no longer do also constitute a warm list if you have correct addresses for them. If your organization gives people advice, referrals, or other service over the phone or through the mail, create a system to gather the names of people served, unless that information is confidential. This list is the least warm because not all the people calling you are donors to anything, you don't know if they were satisfied with what they got from you, and they may feel they deserve to get the information you are giving out for free. However, some will be grateful and want to help, and some will prefer to pay for the information rather than accept it for free. Keep a log of these types of contacts in a database on your computer and merge these every so often to eliminate duplicates and to pull out anyone who is already a donor to create a list of prospects. (If your organization only has one computer or has volunteers who are not used to using a database, use the old-fashioned method of writing down names and addresses either on a list or directly onto envelopes.) When people call, respond to their request and then ask if you can send them more information about your organization. Make sure you tell people your Web site address, and make sure your site also encourages giving. People who don't want an appeal will decline to give their address. Some of these people will go to your Web site later and become donors. Names from information requests that come through the mail can be transferred directly onto carrier envelopes; every time you have compiled two hundred envelopes you can send an appeal by bulk mail. Some groups prefer to send appeals by first-class mail as the names come in. This ensures a hotter prospect, as people are more likely to open first-class mail, and they are receiving the mailing much closer to the time they have been in touch with you, but mailing first class is obviously more expensive than sending by bulk mail. Renting and Trading Lists The other type of warm lists are lists of people who belong to organizations that are similar to yours. To get these names requires renting or trading mailing lists. No one actually buys a mailing list outright. By renting it, they acquire the right to use the list one time. Many organizations with large or specialized mailing lists rent their lists as an income stream. You may have noticed that if you give to one organization you will receive appeals from several similar organizations within a few weeks. Your name has been rented because you are a proven "buyer" through direct mail. You rent mailing lists either from a mailing list broker or from another organization. Professional mailing list brokers have a wide variety of lists available, which are *used by both nonprofit organizations and businesses. Most brokers will send you a free catalogue of the categories of names available and the number of names in each category. The variety is astounding. A quick glance through one catalogue shows these possible offerings: sports medicine doctors, corporate secretaries in corporations with budgets greater than $250,000, earthquake research engineers, season ticket-holders to dance performances, donors to animal shelters, women in the press, or even the fascinating category, super-wealthy women (a list of 236,000 names nationally). These lists come to you in ZIP-code order. The lists generally cost $75 to $125 per thousand names, with a minimum rental of two thousand to five thousand names. For a small additional fee, you can have lists crossed with each other, yielding the names, for example, of all the super-wealthy women who are donors to animal shelters or of earthquake engineers who are donors to historic preservation projects. A caution here: grassroots groups often assume that people in lucrative occupations (doctors, lawyers, stockbrokers) will be generous donors. This is not the case—there has to be some evidence that the people on list of doctors you have rented are also interested in your issue. Also, just because someone is in a lucrative profession and gives to other charities, they are not necessarily worth your direct mail investment. Be judicious in using rented lists. To find mailing list brokers, look in the Yellow Pages under Mailing Houses, Mailing List Brokers, or Fundraising Services and Consultants. Also, ask organizations that use direct mail services for their recommendations. Many low-budget organizations trade mailing lists with other organizations for a one-time use. Usually, lists are traded on a name-for-name basis: two hundred names for two hundred names and on up. A group can also trade names for as many names as they have and rent the rest. If your organization has five hundred donors and you want another group's list of two thousand donors, trade your five hundred and pay for the remaining fifteen hundred. Depending on your relationship with the other organization, it may rent the list to you simply for the cost of producing the list on labels or the cost of the labels plus handling, or it may seek to make some profit. If you almost never rent your list, each of your names may be worth between two and five names of an organization that rents their list more often. If you have a mailing list of two hundred donor names that you have never rented out before, you may be able to trade for a list of one thousand. Dos and Don'ts of Sharing Lists Organizations often feel reluctant to share their donor lists with other organizations. One fear is that their donors will prefer the other groups and stop giving or give less to their group. Studies of donors show that this is not true. In fact, donor loyalty to the first group they give to in a series of organizations with related goals is increased as they learn of similar organizations. In other* *words, if a person gives to an environmental organization and then is solicited by several others, he or she may think, "I already support a group that does good work on the environment," or "I've been concerned about environmental degradation for a long time, and it's good that a lot of groups are working on it." Furthermore, most people who give to charity give to a number of them—usually between five and eleven. Often, most of the charities are similar: they may all be arts organizations or environmental groups, or they may be civil rights and civil liberties causes, but there will be some similar theme in all the charities. People change one or two charities each year,*

dropping one and taking on a new one. You are going to lose some donors every year (about one-third), but you will not lose donors simply by sharing your list. To ensure that the names of donors who might take offense at being solicited by organizations other than yours are excluded from your rented lists, simply include a line in your newsletter or on your reply device that says, "From time to time we make our mailing list available to other organizations that we feel would be of interest to our members. If you would rather we did not include your name, please drop us a line (or check here on the form) and we will make sure that you do not receive any of these mailings." You can publish this announcement in every issue of the newsletter and put it in the subscription form on your Web site to be sure that every donor sees it. Very few people will actually write in with this request, but it is worth it to keep those that do happy. Most people like to get mail, and although they grouse about how much direct mail they get, they also feel important and needed because of the volume of mail that comes to them, and they have too much going on their lives to spend a lot of time and energy being mad about a mail appeal. Do not steal mailing lists or use mailing lists that are marked "members only" or "do not use for solicitation." Because mailing lists are fairly easy to compile and acquire, once you have the systems in place there is no need to be underhanded with others' lists. Further, your organization's reputation may suffer. Almost all mailing lists, particularly those rented from commercial firms, have a certain number of dummy names: names that are placed to identify the use of that list. The letter addressed to a dummy name goes to the source of the list. Suppose you have liberated the list of members of a service club that has given your organization a donation. John Q. Jones is on that list, put there by the service club itself. ("Q" ensures that this is likely an unduplicated name.) When a letter arrives addressed to John Q. Jones, the service club knows it came from their list and will check out whether someone gave your organization permission to use the list. The situation can then become unpleasant and counterproductive to your fundraising efforts. A final rule about list acquisition and development: Do not save mailing lists. On a list that is more than three months old, 7 percent of the addresses will already be inaccurate. After you have used a list twice (if you have permission to do so), you have gotten 90 percent of the response you are going to get from that list. Concentrate your efforts on getting new names and refine your systems so that the names are as hot as possible. The quality of the list is pivotal to your direct mail success.

7

Fundraising by phone

With the predictability of gravity, I always know that when I get to the part of a training or consultation where I recommend using the phone, I am going to get more pushback than from almost any other strategy. People invariably say, "I hate being phoned.""I always hang up right away.""I would never give to an organization that phoned me." But usually after four or five expostulations on the evils of phoning, someone (often someone under thirty-five) will say, "I gave over the phone just the other night when the library called." "So did I," says someone else. At that point usually one of the people who never gives by phone says, "Well, that's different—that's the library. I gave to them also." We laugh and move on to explore the wide world of dialing for dollars. For many years, telemarketing grew and grew, and although it was very unpopular, it did work with a large cross section of the population. In 2003, Congress passed one of the most popular pieces of legislation ever, the "Do Not Call Act." You can now opt out of receiving telemarketing calls just by registering your phone number with a master "Do Not Call" list. Nonprofits are exempt from the Do Not Call list. Do Not Call has decreased the volume of calls phenomenally, actually making the environment more friendly to callers from nonprofits. Phoning works. Phone-a-thons continue to result in a greater percentage of response than direct mail, and they are an excellent way of reaching a large number of people with a (somewhat) personal message. Like direct mail, phone-a-thons can be modified for small organizations in a way that allows them both to raise money and not offend donors. The two modifications small organizations make are to use very warm lists (such as lapsed and current donors, friends of board members, staff, and current donors, or lists of donors to similar organizations) and to use volunteers to do the calling. Even if a person is annoyed to be phoned during dinner, they will be less annoyed by a volunteer who is giving their time and doesn't sound as smooth as a professional telemarketer. A basic fundraising axiom is that the closer you can get to the prospect, the more likely you are to get the gift. Phoning, as a telephone company ad used to say, is "the next best thing to being there." BASIC TECHNIQUE OF THE PHONE-A-THON In its simplest terms, a phone-a-thon involves a group of volunteers calling people to ask them to support your organization with a donation. A phone-a-thon is an excellent way to involve volunteers in fundraising because it teaches them how to ask for money in a way that they may find less intimidating than soliciting donations in face-to-face situations. Phone-a-thons can be good moneymakers. They are usually inexpensive to produce and have a high rate of return. Between 5 and 10 percent of the people reached will contribute, possibly more when calling lapsed donors to renew their gifts and definitely more when calling current donors about a specific campaign. The costs involved include printing and postage, any toll-call charges, and food and drinks for volunteers doing the calling. If you haven't already, arrange for your organization to be able to accept credit card donations. You will get larger gifts and have a smaller loss of pledges using credit cards. (See Chapter Nineteen for more on accepting gifts by credit card.) A phone-a-thon can be organized by one or two people. It takes several hours of preparation followed by a five-hour block of time for the event. Several people are needed to make all the calls (for how to determine how many people, see the formula below). Preparation To prepare for a phone-a-thon, the organizers take the following eight steps: Step 1. Prepare the List. Make a list of people who will be called. These potential donors are people who have either expressed an interest in your organization, have benefited by something you have done for them, or are past or current supporters of your organization. People attending community meetings you have organized, alumnae, and members of and donors to similar organizations are all prospects. Get their names and look up their phone numbers. (Organizations in small towns or rural communities or organizations that serve a specific neighborhood or geographic constituency may be able to use the phone book as their source of names, but generally this is too cold a list.) Create a master list of prospects to be called, either by using a computer-based spreadsheet or a handwritten list with columns for names, phone numbers, codes indicating the person's relationship to the organization (L = lapsed, FB = former board member, CL = client, and so on), and any information it would be helpful for the telephone volunteer to have, as in the following illustration. The list will also have a column for recording whether the prospect made a donation and for how much, which will be filled in after the calling is completed.

If the only phone number you have for a person is known to be for a cell phone, it's best not to call, especially when calling for acquisition. When you have a choice of a home phone or cell phone, use the home phone. If you know that a former donor, board member, or alumnus does not have a land line, you can call their cell phone. When reaching someone on a cell phone, it is particularly imperative to ask whether this is a good time to talk and to be willing to call back or be called back when the person is at a better point (for example not driving) to talk. Step 2. Create a File Record or Card for Each Prospect. The volunteers will use these cards (see illustration) to record the result of the phone call. After the calls have been made and these cards are filled in, you can use them to check off the names on the master list and record whether a donation was made and the amount. Step 3. Set a Date for the Phone-A-Thon. When looking for a date, pay attention to other events in your community. Don't call, for example, on an evening when everyone will be at an anniversary party or benefit auction for another group. Most people find that calling on a Tuesday, Wednesday, or Thursday night between 6 P.M. and 9 P.M. at the beginning of the month (near payday) works best. Some groups call on weekends with success, but calling on a sunny weekend afternoon may bring people racing in from their yard or interrupt them while entertaining and may irritate more people than necessary. No one is sitting in the sun on a Wednesday evening at 8:00 P.M. Pay attention as well to what's on television: don't call during the Superbowl, on an election night, or during the Academy Awards. Step 4. Write a Script. Generally, volunteers can ad lib after the second or third call, but initially a script of what to say gives them a feeling of security. The script should be brief and to the point, as in the following sample. SAMPLE PHONE-A-THON SCRIPT "Hello, my name is Jill Activist, and I am a volunteer with Good Organization. May I speak with you for a minute?" (Pause for answer.)

8

Fundraising by Internet

The fastest-growing area of fundraising in the world is on the Internet. Online giving, using e-mail to keep in touch with donors and even to solicit donations, and organizational blogs and e-newsletters are in wide use. However, the Internet has also proved to be disappointing to a large number of grassroots organizations that saw visions of sugar plums if they only built a fancy Web site or started an e-newsletter. Although some organizations raise $100,000 or more every year online, dozens more report getting only a handful of new donors using the same technology. So what should a small, probably never-going-to-be-famous organization do with regard to the Internet and fundraising? How much should such a group invest and what kind of returns should they look for? Although references to using the Internet occur throughout this book, this chapter focuses more specifically on using a Web site for fundraising. I must confess at the outset that, either by generation or temperament or both, I find the kind of communication that other (often younger) people take for granted—text messages, instant messaging, e-vites—still feels new to me and not that interesting. I find e-mail to be in equal parts helpful and bothersome. I'd rather pick up the phone than send an e-mail, I dislike instant messaging, and I have never sent a text message. My personal virtual preferences may provide a clue to those of many others and a warning not to assume universal familiarity or ease with the technology on the part of your donors. There are two other considerations as well: first, everything in this chapter runs the risk of being outdated almost before the book is published; and second, there is a clear digital divide between large or high-profile nonprofits and small, grassroots nonprofits. Figuring out how much time and energy an organization with one or two beleaguered staff and an already highly involved group of volunteers should put into expanding their Web presence is tricky and will vary from organization to organization.

All that notwithstanding, I do recognize that there are wonderful opportunities on the Internet for fundraising, and every organization, regardless of how tiny or rural, can and should take advantage of what the Internet has to offer. Of course, as with all fundraising, anything you do on the Internet needs to be part of a larger plan, coordinated with all other communication, and integrated with your programs. That there are no stand-alone strategies is quite obvious with the Internet. The advantages of the Internet are clear. More than sixty million Americans use e-mail every week, and about half that many surf the Web. Of the 80 percent of private-sector funding donated by individuals, giving through the Internet accounts for an exponentially increasing number of donations, particularly gifts in the $35 to $250 range. Some organizations report that gifts given over the Internet are larger than those given by direct mail. Giving online is growing by leaps and bounds; many Internet experts predict that as much as 40 percent of small donations will be made online within the next five years. Knowing how to attract, and more important, keep donors online is a new science and we learn more about how to do this every day. I encourage you to go online and see all the information that is available. (See Resource E, For Further Information, for a number of helpful Web sites and books about fundraising on the Internet.) For many nonprofits, organizing and fundraising via the World Wide Web is tailor-made for a culture that increasingly expects everything to be available all the time. The Web is a 24/7 proposition (available twenty-four hours a day, seven days a week) that allows your organization to be "open" across time zones and international boundaries even when your office is not. The digital divide between rich and poor decreases daily as corporate and individual donors make sure that libraries and schools are outfitted with the latest technology. Internet access at senior centers, community centers, and Internet cafes makes access to the Internet possible across all class, race, and age lines and means Internet access is almost universal. In fact, one of the fastest-growing populations of Internet users is senior citizens. The divide is far from over, however, and organizations serving poor and rural communities have a different experience—even of the use of e-mail—than organizations in larger communities.

THE ABSOLUTE NECESSITIES To take advantage of the fundraising capabilities of the Internet, there are some things you must have: e-mail and high-speed service, your own domain name, and your own Web site. E-Mail and High-Speed Service The vast majority of even tiny nonprofits now have e-mail; if you don't have it, you need to get it. Not having e-mail puts you at almost the same disadvantage as not having a telephone. Further, you need to have high-speed

Internet access rather than dial-up, unless high-speed access—via satellite, cable, or DSL—is not available in your community. The time you waste waiting to get online with a dial-up service costs you far more than the monthly cost of a high-speed service. Your Own Domain Name You also need your own domain name—that is, the name by which you are recognized on the Internet. A domain name costs between $100 and $150 per year and allows you to build a consistent brand and to promote the name of your organization. If for some reason the name of your organization is not available as a domain name, then use a phrase that will remind people of your work. "Youthforchange" or "Homesforall" or something close to your organization's name and message will work for a domain name. Your Own Web Site A Web site is almost as imperative as e-mail, but it needs to be conceptualized as part of your communications plan. Just to take some obvious examples, the logo on your Web site needs to be the same as the logo on your letterhead. Just as you think about the audience you are writing to in a direct mail appeal or who will come to your special event, you need to think about who is going to use your Web site and tailor it to that audience. Look at the Web sites of organizations that are similar to yours and see what they have done. Don't try to save money by building a site cheaply or using someone to build the site who understands only the technology and not the marketing of Web sites. Hiring a Web designer is a good investment. Designing a Web site can cost almost any amount of money, but be prepared to spend at least $500. As you budget for it, think about what you get with a Web site—anyone in the whole world who has access to the Internet can now find out about your organization. Many people will never visit you in person; this will be their only impression of you. A Web presence and Web strategy can easily cost $5,000 even for a small organization, so this is a project you might want to approach your major donors to underwrite. Many sophisticated donors understand the need for a high-quality Internet presence and will help you with an extra gift. Dropping unprofitable fundraising strategies and freeing up the money to focus on your Web site is another way to pay for it. Many groups have found the money for their site simply by eliminating people from their mailing list who have never donated or haven't made a gift in several years. One organization with a mailing list of ten thousand and a donor base of two thousand dropped five thousand names from their list after they figured out that it was costing them $2 per person per year to keep those nondonors on the list. They invested the $10,000 they saved into creating and maintaining what is now a successful Web site. Of course, having a Web site is not like having a refrigerator or having a painting, where the initial investment is almost all the money you are going *to spend. A Web site is actually more like the laundry—you no sooner catch up with the laundry than you are behind again. The site needs new content at least monthly, and it will need to be redesigned every few years. These are expenses you must plan for. Most small organizations find that having a talented freelance webmaster is the best solution. Some organizations have an in-house webmaster whose job is to maintain the organization's Web presence as well as manage other communications and publications. Most organizations that I work with have a Web site, and in many cases their sites are pretty good. However, they are often lacking one critical detail, which is a "donate now" icon on the home page and on as many other pages as possible. The "donate now" button can take a user to a page that they download, fill out, and send in with a check the old-fashioned way. However, if you accept credit cards—and doing so is something you should explore—figure out how to have people become donors online using their credit card. One way to be able to accept credit cards is through a service such as Network for Good or Groundspring, nonprofits that exist to collect donations for other nonprofits and that can handle credit card donations and even pledges. If you anticipate a high enough volume or you sell products and services on your site as well as accept donations, you will want to explore having your own system.*

DRIVING TRAFFIC TO YOUR SITE Part of the planning for your site is determining who it is for and how you are going to get these people to visit it. This is called "driving traffic" to the site; it is the difference between a merely well-designed site and a successful one. There are literally billions of Web sites in the world, and some of the nicest ones remain unknown and unvisited because no one thinks to look for them. There are some simple and low-cost ways to drive traffic to your site. Make sure your Web address is on everything you publish—your business cards, your e-mail signature, your letterhead, your newsletter (in several places, often as a footer on the bottom of each page)—and that it is part of your voice mail message and on any information you give out about your organization. Register with all the key search engines: Yahoo, Google, and the like (find a list of current search engines at www.searchenginewatch.com). Further, ask your webmaster to make sure that your "meta tag" and "title"—two items hidden at the top of the code for your site—have as many relevant words as possible so that search engines can index your site. Get help thinking through the two- or three-word title for your organization that will show up in a Web search as a description of your organization and that you want people to click on to come to your Web site. For example, if I type your issue and the town I live in into Google or another search engine, your site should come up in the results, preferably at or near the top of the list. The three words that will be used in the sentence that describes your group need to be accurate and interesting so that I will want to click on them and go to your homepage. Make sure that any directories of nonprofits, service providers, chambers of commerce, and so on list your Web site along with your postal address. Link to other organizations and make sure they link to you. Make a list of organizations you would see as allies or as offering complementary information to yours and make sure that people can go to their sites from yours and viceversa. Every so often visit related sites and see what they say about you. E-mail is one of the best ways to get people to visit your site. A simple and easy thing to do is to gather as many e-mail addresses of donors as you can and send them an e-mail newsletter or e-mail alert each month or quarter. You can use this communication to announce new content on your site or to suggest action, about which they learn more details by going to your site from a link in the e-mail message.

As with all fundraising strategies, never promise on the front end what you can't deliver on the back end. If you say your e-newsletter is quarterly, it has to come out quarterly and not twice a year! I have signed up for more than a dozen e-newsletters and never gotten them. On the other hand, I am on lists of e-newsletters that I never signed up for. It does not make sense to add someone to your list who hasn't asked to be on it, and it really doesn't make sense not to add people when they have used your Web site to sign up. Be sure that "fulfillment"—the cost in time and money to fulfill promises made—is built into to all your planning. USES OF E-MAIL E-mail can be used in a variety of ways to help build and maintain a donor base, including e-newsletters, correspondence with donors, and keeping board members and volunteers up to date. E-Mail Newsletters Some organizations simply post their paper newsletter on their Web site. Other organizations have done away with paper newsletters altogether and only send e-newsletters. Neither of these decisions is proving to be wise. E-newsletters and paper newsletters are actually quite different. An e-newsletter is much shorter, both overall and in each story, than a printed newsletter. In an e-newsletter, you tell a short version of the story, then provide a hyperlink that takes readers to your Web site for more information. An e-mail newsletter generally emphasizes different information than your paper newsletter, and you hope some cross section of donors will read both. For these reasons, e-newsletters and paper newsletters need to be conceptualized as different forms of communication. Having only an e-newsletter can decrease your visibility to donors, since that kind of newsletter is far too easily deleted from a long list of e-mail.

E-mail is especially effective for posting information alerts or calls to action—anything that requires an instant response. And unlike paper, to send one *hundred thousand messages by e-mail costs no more than sending one or one hundred. Corresponding with Donors You can also use e-mail to correspond with donors (although do not use it as the only way you send thank you notes). When you leave a message for a donor on the phone, leave both your phone number and your e-mail address as a way to get back to you. There are more and more instances of an entire solicitation being done online, with a commitment to a gift given by e-mail. E-mail can be used in the place of an introductory postal letter—in fact it can be used most places where you might have used postal mail, with one caveat: it is still worth the personal touch to send handwritten (if possible) thank you notes through the postal mail (for more on thanking people, see Chapter Seventeen). E-mail is a great way to send short notes to major donors during the year, keeping them posted on things you think they would find of interest. The savings in dollars and time of maintaining relationships by e-mail is one of its great benefits. Working with the Board and Volunteers E-mail is an excellent way to keep board members and volunteers posted on internal happenings that would be interesting to them but would not go in a general newsletter. Many groups use e-mail to encourage board member efforts in fundraising with notes like this: "Update on Major Donor Campaign. Eric Johnson just concluded a request for $1,000 and the donor is sending it today. He is following up with three other prospects. Martha was finally able to set up a meeting with the two donors who may give us $10,000 on Tuesday. Keep your fingers crossed. Earlyse is the leader in number of gifts so far—five at $250 and four at $100! Good work, everyone!" Some organizations have created an internal listserv of board and staff members, enabling any of them to post information to the group. Some organizations have a member listserv, where any member can ask a question, give advice, or announce upcoming events. This feature is particularly useful in coalitions or associations of several organizations. In this situation, someone needs to moderate the listserv to make sure that one or two people don't dominate or that the content stays focused. Some organizations are also taking advantage of blogging, a form of communication that was originally a personal posting of a diary or a journal (known as a Web log). Most of us are familiar with blogs that are sent by friends who are traveling to fun and interesting places or are having some other kinds of adventures they want to share with a number of people and are willing to have read by anyone who comes across the blog. Executive directors, board chairs, and sometimes program staff are now starting blogs reflecting on various aspects of their work and their personal feelings and thoughts about it. Blogs can come out as frequently or infrequently as the person wants, as they don't carry the expectation of regularity* *that a newsletter implies. Further, a blog can contain much more emotional content and often creates a different and sometimes deeper relationship with readers than a newsletter. People can respond to blogs, so they also can be a way of testing an idea.*

RECEIVING DONATIONS AND PAYMENT ONLINE There are two ways to receive donations online: by creating a secure area on your Web site where people can make donations or purchases, or by using a charity portal to handle payment transactions for you. Creating a Secure Area If your organization already has the capacity to accept donations via credit cards and electronic fund transfers, and you have items for sale or you can expect to receive a number of donations through your Web site, you will want to have a "secured area" on your site where people can key in their credit card number to donate or buy online with the assurance that their transaction is safe (by being encrypted before it is transmitted). Many organizations have found receiving donations or making sales this way to be extremely lucrative, but it also adds a layer of work. Someone has to download the orders and fill them. The site has to be programmed to send an automated reply message acknowledging the order or donation. Credit card numbers have to be processed. All of this work will be worth it as the site gets more traffic and more donations come in, but there is an initial investment that may take a while to pay off. Charity Portals Another way to receive donations or fees for goods is by using what's known as a charity portal. These are Web sites run by both for-profit and nonprofit groups that list a variety of charities on a site, with a description of each charity and a way to donate to each one. The theory is that there are people wanting to give money who do not have a way to find groups that meet their values. These people would go to a charity portal, look under "children," or "environment," or whatever they care most about and find names and descriptions of groups they can give to. When they donate, the sponsor of the portal takes a small percentage of the donation and sends the rest to the specified charity. Some portals are designed to let people buy products, then donate a portion of the sale to a charity. If you decide to register your group with a portal, try to choose one that is itself a nonprofit. A nonprofit portal is less likely to advertise to your donors or to sell information they have gleaned about your donors to other advertisers. Make sure you know what you get from being registered and what the costs are. Also, make sure you will be sent the names and addresses of the donors and not just the money the donors sent. Some donors have been disgruntled to learn that the charity they chose never knew who they were, but that their name was sold to other Internet companies or catalog companies wanting to expand their pool of potential customers. Remember that above all, you want people coming to your Web site, where they can be invited to make a donation. Anything you do, including being listed on another site, needs to lead to that end. NO MIRACLE, BUT ANOTHER STRATEGY TO EXPLORE The Internet is neither a miracle cure to your fundraising problems nor something to be suspicious of. It is simply another strategy. It appeals to a younger, generally well-educated and possibly affluent group of people. It appeals to people who feel that they have little or no time. Through search engines, it allows people who may have never heard of your group to find out about it. The Internet can be used to build a certain kind of feeling of belonging on the part of people who may never make it to your office or to an event you put on. Using the Internet effectively requires an ongoing investment of time and money. For organizations that make that investment and don't try to short-circuit the process, it can be worth the effort.

9
Building Major Gifts

The financial payoff for all fundraising is receiving large gifts from some of your donors. To build a major donor program, no matter the size of the organization, a majority of staff, board, and volunteers must feel comfortable asking people for money in person. (See Chapter Six, Getting Comfortable with Asking for Money.) For many people, that comfort starts with being able to ask someone for $10 for a ticket to a benefit event such as a dance or for $35 to become a member. Some people never move past that level of comfort, but if an organization is to grow and thrive, a critical mass of board, volunteers, and staff must be able to ask for much larger gifts—$500, $5,000, $50,000, and even more. A person doesn't have to like asking for money to be able to do it. Some of the most successful fundraisers I have known have confessed that they always feel anxious when asking for money. But they do it anyway, and sometimes their nervousness makes them prepare more thoroughly for the solicitation and feel even better about themselves and their group after they complete it. Once an organization is in the habit of asking for large gifts, it quickly moves to needing a more systematic plan for soliciting such gifts. That system is a major gifts program. Some groups prefer to do their major donor fundraising in the form of a campaign; major gifts campaigns are discussed in Chapter Twenty-Three. Before beginning a major gifts program, your organization must make a number of decisions: how much money it wishes to raise from large gifts, the minimum amount that will constitute a major gift (in this book it is $250), how many gifts of what size are needed. In addition, you must decide what, if any, tangible benefits donors will receive for their gifts and what materials will be needed for the solicitors. Finally, a core group of volunteers must be trained to ask for the gifts. SETTING A GOAL The first step in seeking major gifts is to decide how much money you want to raise from major donors. This amount will be related to the overall amount you *want to raise from all your individual donors and can be partly determined based on the following information. (For more on goal setting, see Chapter Thirty-Nine, Creating a Fundraising Plan.) Over the years fundraisers have observed the following pattern of how gifts come into healthy organizations: · 60 percent of the income comes from 10 percent of the donors · 20 percent of the income comes from 20 percent of the donors · 20 percent of the income comes from 70 percent of the donors In other words, the majority of your gifts will be small, but the bulk of your income will come from large donations. Based on that pattern, it is possible to project for any fundraising goal how many gifts of each size you should seek and how many prospects you will need to ask to get each gift. For example, if your organization must raise $50,000 from grassroots fundraising, you should plan to raise $30,000 (60 percent) from major gifts, mostly solicited personally; $10,000 (20 percent) from habitual donors, mostly solicited through phone, mail, and regular special events; and $10,000 from people giving for the first or second time, solicited from mail and online appeals, speaking engagements, special events, product sales, and the like. If you have 500 donors, then, expect that about 50 of them will be major donors, about 100 of them will be habitual donors, and about 350 will be first- or second-time donors or donors who give small gifts every year, but for whom your organization is not a high priority. The lowest major gift you request should be an amount that is higher than most of your donors give but one that most employed people can afford, especially if allowed to pledge. Even many low-income people can afford $25 a month or $250 a quarter, which brings being a major donor into the realm of possibility for all people close to your group. Some organizations try to avoid setting goals. Their feeling is that they will raise as much as they can from as many people as they can. This doesn't work. Prospects are going to ask how much you need; if this answer is, "As much as we can get," your group will not sound very well run. If prospects think a group will simply spend whatever it has, they will give less than they can afford or nothing. Further, without a goal there is no way to measure how well the organization is doing compared to its plans. Just as you wouldn't instruct a builder to build a house that will be "as big as it needs to be," or "as big as we can afford," you can't build a donor base with vague or meaningless assertions. APPORTIONMENT OF GIFTS It would be great if you could say, "Well, we need $40,000 from 10 percent of our donors, so that will mean two hundred people giving $200 each." But two hundred people will not all behave the same way—some will give more, most will give less. Based on this reality, fundraisers have made a second observation: for the money needed annually from individual donors, you need one gift equal to 10 percent or more of the goal, two gifts equal to 10 percent (5 percent each) or* *more of the goal, and four to six gifts providing the next 10 percent of the goal. The remaining gifts needed are determined in decreasing size of gift with increasing numbers of gifts. Using this formula, you can create what is called a Gift Range Chart or a Gift Pyramid.*

Benefits First, you need to decide what, if any, benefits people will receive for giving a major gift. While helping the organization is the main satisfaction for the donor, an added incentive, such as a mug, an invitation to a special reception, or a T-shirt, will show that you appreciate the extra effort the donor is making and will remind the donor of their gift to your group. There is no evidence that one kind of benefit works better than another (see also the discussion of benefits in Chapter Ten). Certainly, the benefit should not be very expensive. Under IRS law, any value of a benefit that exceeds the vague criterion of "token" is not eligible for the same tax deduction as the rest of the gift. For example, if someone gives $500 to an organization and receives an etching worth $50, the donor can only claim $450 of this gift on their tax return because $50 is more than a token amount. If the same group gave a T-shirt or tote bag worth little or nothing on the open market, the donor could claim the whole $500 as a tax deduction. The IRS is increasingly questioning expensive benefits for donors. The benefit should be easy to mail, which is why many groups use T-shirts or books as benefits. Because of the number of items people can commonly get for their gifts to public television, libraries, or major national organizations, a small organization should probably offer something that is related to its programs. For example, an organization working for stricter controls on and alternatives to the commercial use of pesticides sends its major donors a short booklet on alternatives to pesticides for home gardens and indoor plants. An after-school program for inner-city children aged eight to eleven asked the teachers to save drawings the children made that they didn't want to take home. The organization sent the best of those artworks along with their thank you notes to donors. This benefit is truly of token value, but it is very popular with donors. Now the organization has one day on which the children are asked to make "thank you" drawings. A major donor program can be run successfully without giving any benefits beyond what are offered to all donors, such as the newsletter. This approach will only work if the donors are thanked personally and promptly and if the organization keeps in touch with them using the ways recommended in the section on renewing major gifts later in this chapter. Personal attention and information on what work the group was able to do as a result of their gift will always be more effective in maintaining donors than any nominal benefits. Materials that describe your program are the second element needed for soliciting *major donations. An organization should have a well-designed, easy-to-understand brochure. It does not have to be elaborate or printed in several colors, but it should be professionally laid out, well written, and free of grammatical and typographical errors. Because this pamphlet will be used primarily in personal solicitation, it should focus on ways to make thoughtful gifts. For example, if you have an electronic funds transfer program or a pledge program, or if you accept credit cards or you are seeking gifts of stocks and bonds, you can explain all that in the brochure. The brochure is a published version of your case statement (see Chapter Four). It also helps volunteer solicitors by giving them something to leave with a donor and to refer to if they forget some information they meant to impart. Return envelopes and return cards must be included with the brochure. A version of this brochure should also appear on your Web site, with the option for people to donate online. Solicitors Finally, you need to have a core group of people willing to do the soliciting. Some of these people should be from the board of directors, but the board's work can be augmented by a group of volunteers. These people should be trained in the process of asking for money (see Chapters Six and Seven). They do not have to have previous experience in asking for major gifts, nor do they need to know many prospects personally. But they must be donors—ideally, major donors—themselves. KEEPING IN TOUCH WITH MAJOR DONORS One of the most frequent complaints from major donors is that organizations treat them like ATMs—they punch in the amount they want and then walk away until they need money again. To keep donors interested in your group requires showing some interest in the donor, particularly some interest in why the donor is interested in your group. To give major donors this extra attention takes work, but it is worth it for several reasons: first, courtesy; second, because it brings donors closer to the work of your group, making them potential activists or advocates; and third, because it will bring in more money. You should be in contact with your major donors two or three times a year in addition to the time when you ask the donors to renew their gifts. You will want to be in touch with some donors more often than that, depending partly on the size of their gift and mostly on their personality and expressed level of interest. Remember that major donors are a good source of feedback, advice, and volunteer energy, as well as a source of other major donors. There are several easy ways to keep in touch with major donors that make them feel personally appreciated and do not cost the organization much in time or money. You can choose from the suggestions here or develop your own system, but be sure to get a system in place. Send a Holiday Card During December. The card should wish the donor happy holidays and be signed by the chair of the board, a board member with a personal relationship* to the donor, or a staff person. If possible, write a brief note on the card. The card goes alone—no return envelope, no appeal letter. (You may also send major donors a year-end appeal in a separate mailing.) Unless your organization is religiously identified, make sure the card has no religious overtones, including cultural Christian overtones such as Santa Claus, elves, or Christmas trees. The same applies to the postage stamp you choose. Attach a Personal Note to Your Annual Report. All donors should receive a copy of your annual report. Those going to major donors should have a personal note attached. The note can be on a Post-it and does not have to be long. It says something like, "Thought you'd be interested in seeing this since you have been so important to our success," or "I hope you are as proud of our work as we are— your gift helped make it possible." It doesn't matter if you don't know the donor— a personal note shows that they are appreciated. If you know that something in your report will be of particular interest, note that: "Paul, that program you asked about is featured on page five," or "Fran, check out the photo on the back inside cover." Staff usually write these notes, but again, board members with relationships to these donors can write them as well. Report Successes During the Year. If you have positive press coverage, if you win a victory in your organizing or litigation efforts, if you are commended by a community group, service club, or politician, take the opportunity to send a special letter to major donors telling them of the event. If possible, include a copy of the article or commendation. This letter does not have to be personalized.

Note a Donor's Accomplishments. If you know a donor's birthday, send a card. If you learn that someone graduated from college, won an award, or had a baby, send a card. Don't spend a lot of time trying to learn this kind of information, but pay attention and respond when the information comes your way. If you have your donor's e-mail address (and you should) you can send e-cards to save postage. Include Brief Personal Notes with All Mailings. You can include a brief note with anything major donors will be getting anyway, such as invitations to special events or announcements of meetings. Include Major Donors in Some General Mailings. Although you will not send major donors all the requests for extra gifts that are sent to the rest of your donor base, when a mail appeal is particularly timely or concerns a specific issue that will be interesting to them, include major donors in the mailing. Send a Quick E-Mail. You will be in touch with many of your major donors by e-mail, particularly if you have an e-newsletter. From time to time, drop them a quick e-mail note or forward something that you think they will be interested in seeing. By keeping in touch with your major donors, you will lay the groundwork necessary to approach *them for a renewal of their gift in the second year they give and a request to increase the size of their gift the third year of their giving. Even if no one in your organization has ever met this major donor and their gift came unsolicited, through personal notes and letters you will begin to build a rapport that will make it easy to meet the person in the future.*

10

Segmenting Donor Lists to Build Loyalty

———♡———

I hope it is obvious by now that having a donor is not like having a pillowcase or a table. Donors take maintenance. They are living, breathing beings with feelings and attitudes, and they are being sought by 1.5 million other nonprofits. Certainly, they gravitate to organizations they believe in, but if they have a choice between two organizations they believe in and one pays attention to them and the other doesn't, it is not hard to guess where they will send their money. Segmenting donors basically means figuring out how various cross sections of your donor base like to be asked for money and avoiding using strategies that they don't like or don't respond to. If one donor says she or he hates to be phoned or wants to receive no more than one appeal a year, we tend to think that a huge number of our donors think exactly like this one. I have known organizations that stopped sending multiple appeals because one donor complained, even though fifty donors might have sent in an extra gift! Donors are not all alike. Some dislike being phoned, but others give only by phone. Some will never read an e-newsletter, others will ignore a paper newsletter. One thing donors do have in common is that everyone appreciates thoughtful, personal attention, so we give that to all donors as best we can. Because people have individual likes and dislikes, we should accommodate these preferences when we can. For example, if someone sends your organization $35 with a note that says, "I only give once a year, so please only ask me once a year," code this donor's file in your database to suppress their name for any other mailing during the following twelve months. That person will not be invited to an event or get the spring appeal. Similarly, someone who writes on their reply card, "Absolutely no phone calls" should never be phoned because the information was put in their donor record. In fact, even *if you could take their phone number from their check, don't enter it into your database. If you don't have it, you are much less likely to make a mistake and call. Most donors don't tell us directly what they want. They may still have desires, however, and they indicate their preferences by their behavior. Our goal is to make an informed guess about their behavior before they decide not to give us any more money. Segmenting, which means dividing your donor lists into smaller batches according to various criteria, allows you to take their preferences into account and saves your organization time and money because you are not using strategies with people who have never responded to them. The first set of segments is very simple. Donors should be sorted by how long they have been giving your organization money (longevity), how big their gift is (size), and how often in the same year they make a gift (frequency). Let's look at each of these criteria. Longevity. In many ways, the most important donors are the ones who have given you money for at least three years, regardless of the size of their gift. Create a category for those people. If your organization has been around for a while and your records are good, you may want to create categories for donors who have given for five or even ten or more years. Size. Determine what amount of money is more than most people in your constituency can give, and create a list of donors who give that much or more. In some organizations, this may be $100, but for most it will probably be $250 and up. Frequency. Although there are many donors who give only once a year, there are many others who give every time they are asked. Create a category for people who give two or more times a year. Once you have grouped your donors according to longevity, size, and frequency, print out the following lists of donors: · People who have given $250 (in one gift) more than once a year for three or more years · People who have given $250 once a year for three or more years · People who have given between $100 and $249 once or more than once for three or more years In descending order, these donors are your best prospects for upgrading and are often good people to consider for volunteer opportunities. Your personal solicitation efforts should be directed to these groups. They care about you and have shown that caring for several years. These donors are signaling that they like your organization. Chances are they will respond favorably to personal attention. Show this list to trusted board members, volunteers, and people who know your community and who have some discretion. Ask if they know whether any of the people on these lists are capable of giving a lot more. Perhaps Jane Smith gives you $250 twice a year and has done so for three years. A volunteer knows that Jane Smith gives $1,000 to an organization similar to yours and says that Jane always speaks highly of both organizations. Because as a general rule donors should be asked to upgrade their* *gift every third year, Jane is a little overdue. Your next solicitation to her can ask her to consider making a gift of $500 or even $1,000 (with a good reason for needing that much of an increase, and if the solicitation is done personally). Donors who only give once a year should only be asked once or twice a year, whereas consider sending an extra appeal during the year to people who give every time they are asked; these are also people who should be asked to join a pledge program. People who always renew by phone should no longer get three renewal letters before being phoned; instead, send them one renewal letter and then call them. By observing patterns among your donors, you can save yourself a lot of time and money and increase your fundraising income with little extra work on your part. In addition to categorizing by size, longevity, and frequency, note which donors only come to events or perhaps only come to one event. These donors should not get regular appeal letters unless you have evidence that they respond by giving to those as well. If a donor only gives when she comes to your signature event, does so for three years or more, and does not give to any other appeals, that is a sign that she does not need to get the other appeal letters. If one year that donor does not come to the event, then you could send her a letter after the event telling her how well the event did and how she was missed and asking for a contribution. (Keep in mind that all the donors are getting the newsletter so they can know what is happening at the organization if they want to find out. Segmenting the donors does not mean that some donors never hear from you.)*

Note which donors only give to appeals for specific things (playgrounds, scholarships, capital projects) but who never send money in response to general appeals. If you have a specific need, these are the donors to approach more personally for that need. These are often your best prospects for capital campaigns as well. Identify the people who give several times a year and either send them one more appeal or ask them to become members of a pledge club to see if you can convert them to monthly or quarterly donors. All donors should be offered the chance to pledge on all your reply devices and as a suggestion in renewal letters, but donors who give frequently should be offered that option in a special letter about the advantages of pledging. (For more on setting up a pledge program, see Chapter Nineteen.) Your goal in looking closely at how donors give to your organization is threefold: · You give donors the kind of attention they want · You save the organization from phone calls or letters from frustrated donors saying, "You send too much mail," or "I can't stand being phoned," or "You are using all the money I gave you to ask me for more money" · You are able to focus your primary fundraising energy on donors who are loyal to the organization, as opposed to donors who are loyal to a person in the organization or to an event

STAYING IN TOUCH WITH DONORS In times of economic downturn or world instability, loyal donors are not only the bread and butter but also the lifeblood, to mix metaphors, of an organization. Whatever work you can do to build their loyalty is critical. Matching strategies of asking with types of donors, as described in this chapter, is one way to help build loyalty. Of course asking for money, even in a way the donor responds to, cannot be the only way you are in touch with donors. You need to make sure you are telling the donors what you do and helping them be ambassadors of your work with their friends. Examine all the ways you are in touch with your donors and put yourself in the donor's shoes. If all you knew about an organization was what donors receive, would you as a donor feel proud to be a member of this group? Puzzled? Excited? Would you have a sense of the consistency of your group's work or would it seem scattered?

For example, for three months in a row a monthly newsletter from an organization that works with students in the public schools has printed a number of pictures of young people in political demonstrations. The captions require knowledge that is not provided in the newsletter: "Elkmont High School students protest HR 2233,""Lakeshore Middle School students protest Harris Firing," and "Monument Parents Upset over Locker Room Decision." One has the impression that this organization works primarily through protests and walk-outs around issues that are not common knowledge. Moreover, their thank you notes are generated by computer and merely state, "Thank you so much for your gift of $___. It helps us do our important work improving public education." Although a handful of major donors are sent additional information, mostly because they are also serving in some volunteer capacity, what donors read in the newsletter is all most of them know about the organization's work. When it conducts a small survey of donors, the organization is surprised that no one knows about their tutoring program, or that they are sending ten students to internships in Washington, D.C. These are also exciting program activities that lend themselves to photographs and show much more of the range of the organization's work. The organization rethinks its communications so that each newsletter features an in-depth story on one program area and smaller updates on other programs. The thank you notes are changed so that they also contain a one-paragraph description of one aspect of the work. Not surprisingly, more donations flow in and donors add notes to their reply devices, such as, "Great story about the importance of one-to-one organizing." Read a years' worth of communication from your group and see what you would know and not know about the group's work if that was all you got. You will quickly spot problems and be able to fix them. Further, see if you can add any personalization to your thank you notes *or contact donors with an occasional letter or phone call to show more personal appreciation of their efforts. A letter that begins, "This is the fifth year you have helped us. Let me list some things your gifts have helped make possible over the past five years" is a relatively easy letter to create when seeking renewals. We appreciate all gifts and all motives for giving. But our best chance of getting a donation year in and year out is by building a relationship with the donor— a relationship that goes beyond any of the people in the organization. Segmenting, then deciding how to treat each segment of the donor list, is an easy and important step in building and keeping a broad donor base.*

11

Considering Legacy Giving

Alegacy gift is any donation that requires a lot of thought on the part of the donor. However, we mostly use the term legacy giving (also called planned giving) to refer to arrangements made for a group to receive contributions from the estate of a donor. These gifts are generally made by long-time, loyal donors who believe in the need of the group to exist after their own life is over, and more important, who have faith that the organization will continue to do a good job for years and years to come. These are not necessarily major donors; many bequests come from donors who have given small amounts to an organization for a long time. When I look around at board meetings I attend, I often reflect that in fifty years (which is really very little time), people who aren't even born yet will be running the organization. I will be deceased. What would I need to know about this organization to trust that it will continue to attract people to its board and staff (people who don't exist yet) who will continue to do good and needed work? Whatever information that creates that confidence is fundamental to getting donors to consider legacy gifts. Some organizations use legacy gifts for annual expenses, but since the gift is not repeatable, this practice is unwise. Others use legacy gifts for capital improvements. Most groups, however, use legacy gifts to build endowments. An endowment is a permanently restricted fund invested to generate interest. The principal, or corpus, is never spent but is added to as more legacy gifts come in. The interest income can be used as the organization wishes, unless the donor has created terms restricting how the gift can be used. Interest income is usually used to offset general operating costs, as these are the most difficult to raise money for.

GETTING READY FOR A LEGACY GIVING PROGRAM Many organizations think that getting ready for a legacy giving program involves going to seminars and memorizing complicated financial planning language, then identifying the organization's oldest donors, explaining what you have learned to them, and watching them sign on the dotted line. In fact, before anyone in the organization begins the process of learning the many different ways to word a bequest, a number of things have to be in place. First, it is critical that your organization discusses and agrees on the need to exist far into the future and comes to grips with what that means for your overall mission. Second, in addition to deciding how far into the future your group needs to exist, you need to look at whether people trust you to do your work now and understand your need for funds. Does your group have a good reputation—not just for work accomplished, but for stewarding resources, handling money responsibly, and raising money with integrity? Although many grassroots organizations could answer yes to all these questions, they may be surprised at the extent to which their donors have no sense of how their group deals with money. If you don't put out an annual financial report, if you don't publish the names of your donors from time to time, and if you don't regularly talk about how you raise money, your donors may have never thought much about your financial needs. For example, if someone asks where the local humane society or college or symphony orchestra gets its money, many people would answer that these institutions get a lot of money from individuals and bequests. Because of that, as people write their wills, many think of leaving some of their estate to the humane society or their alma mater or local arts group. You can start a legacy giving program without people being aware of how your organization raises and spends money, but it will not go very far until that information is more commonly known. Third, and closely related to the previous point, you need a donor base that includes people who have given your organization money for several years and who think of your organization as one they will support as long as they can. Many groups need to develop their donor base before they begin a legacy giving program—not just in terms of numbers of donors, but also in terms of donor loyalty. If one or more of these elements are not in place, skip this chapter and re-read the preceding chapters. Do what is recommended in those chapters and you will be ready to come back to legacy giving in a year or two.

PREPARING TO TALK ABOUT LEGACY GIVING Many organizations that have the donor base in place to start a legacy giving program hesitate to do so because of the almost universal taboo about talking about death: not only do people feel awkward talking to anyone about their death, they feel doubly awkward raising the subjects of money and death at same time. Such a discussion may seem not only in bad taste but intrusive. However, it is important to remember that in the United States bequests, which are the most common form of legacy giving, account for nearly 10 percent of all the money given to nonprofits. In fact, the money given from bequests in most years is equal to the money given by foundations and always surpasses the money given by corporations. (An old joke in fundraising is that dead people give away more money than corporations.) If you want people to think of your organization when they are drawing up their estate plans, you will have to ask them in one way or another. When you ask someone for a bequest you are not asking them to die—as inevitable as that will be for us all. You are instead making a statement about your organization and its need, complimenting the donor on their loyalty and commitment to your cause, and giving them another opportunity to act on that commitment. THE IMPORTANCE OF A WILL To give you a sense of the market, more than half of all people die without a will. Of people who make a will, only about 7 percent include a bequest. Even among very wealthy people, for whom a bequest would lower estate tax for their heirs, in the past few years, only 18 percent of estates included bequests. Nonetheless, the vast majority of legacy gifts, regardless of size, are bequests. Fully four out of five planned gifts are made this way, so for many organizations, particularly grassroots ones, establishing a solid bequest program is as far into legacy giving as they will ever need to go. The terms of almost all legacy gifts, even very complicated ones, are laid out in a will. Everyone should have a will because no one knows when they are going to die and because everything you own during your lifetime you also own after your death. You have the authority to direct what happens to your property after you have died, but if you choose not to make a will the state will make that direction for you. Introducing your donors to legacy giving is thus a service to them because it causes them to think about making or updating their wills. Your nonprofit may get some money as a result, but the main service is that making a will protects the donor's family and other interests. If a person dies without a will (called "dying intestate"), the law specifies who will receive the estate, as follows: · If the person is survived by a spouse and not survived by a child or parent, their spouse receives all their property · If a person is survived by a spouse and a parent and not a child, the spouse and parent share the property · If a person is survived by a spouse, child, and a parent, the spouse and child share the property; the parent receives nothing · If a person is not survived by a spouse or a child or a parent, then their brothers and sisters and the children of any deceased brothers and sisters share the person's property.

12

Setting Up an Endowment

During boom years, even the smallest group can be found putting money away into an endowment, a reserve fund, or just a savings account. This money is invested in mutual funds or certificates of deposit and with a little tending, the principal grows, sometimes dramatically. Endowment income is a reliable part of an organization's annual needs, and for organizations with large endowments, the endowment gains can be a major part of income. During bust years and dramatic stock market downturns, putting money aside is less popular. Just as a family or an individual saves for retirement or hard times, any organization that possibly can should put some money aside. Organizations that should be permanent fixtures in the nonprofit landscape need to start endowments. There are ways to invest safely and to ensure both long-term growth and some income. ENDOWMENT DEFINED An endowment is a permanent savings account for an institution. Money is put aside as principal and a small percentage of that principal (traditionally 5 percent) is used for the annual needs of the institution. In years when the principal increases more than 5 percent, the value of the overall endowment increases accordingly, which then increases the amount the organization can use while still staying at the 5 percent figure. In years when the principal does not increase by 5 percent, the organization can still take out 5 percent of the assets without truly eroding the original principal. On the other hand, during huge market downturns, even the original principal may lose value; taking out any of it for operating expenses is not as useful at those times, as doing so further lowers the endowment's value. Using a mix of investments, an endowment can generally weather market instability and still be productive. Like any source of money, an endowment can lose value or even disappear, which is why organizations have to have diversified income streams so that the investment income from an endowment is not critical to survival. BENEFITS OF

ENDOWMENTS Though the advantages of endowments may seem obvious, let's review them: · Just like a savings account, an endowment provides a measure of financial security and takes some of the anxiety out of annual fundraising. · An endowment allows, indeed forces, an organization to think in terms of long-range planning, because an endowment implies a commitment to exist in perpetuity. · An endowment provides a vehicle for people to make larger gifts to an organization than might be appropriate as an annual gift, and an endowment allows people to make one-time-only gifts with the assurance that the gift won't be spent right away. · An endowment gives people a way to express their commitment to an organization through their wills; few people will leave money to an organization that does not have some kind of permanent fund. (See Chapter Twenty-One for more on wills.) · An endowment attracts donors who perceive it to be a sign of good planning and long-range thinking in an organization. · Principal from an endowment can be used for capital expenses (such as a building purchase) and as collateral for loans, if ever needed. In extreme circumstances, the endowment can be used to keep the organization afloat until it can generate other income. (While what's called "invading principal" is something organizations try not to do, there are circumstances in which it might be the best or only recourse, and it is nice to know you have that possibility.) DISADVANTAGES OF ENDOWMENTS Believe it or not, endowments have some drawbacks, too. · If an endowment is big enough, it allows an organization that should have gone out of business, or at least changed the way it works, to exist permanently and to stay the same.

· The income from a large endowment can allow organizations to become unresponsive to their constituency. · Philosophically, money in an endowment has been diverted from the tax stream but is not being used directly for tax-exempt activities. Organizations that are troubled by decreasing support from government funding and increasing privatization of services they believe the government should be providing with tax dollars will need to grapple with this dilemma. · As we have seen in the first years of this century, endowments can provide a false sense of security. Interest rates vary, stock markets crash, and of course, money can always be invested badly. · The existence of an endowment may discourage some donors from giving who prefer to support organizations that they perceive to need the money more. On the other hand, some donors may choose to give to an endowment rather than to annual operating costs. · As with any large source of money earmarked for a specific program, endowments that are linked to certain programs can cause the work of the organization to become driven by the donor's stipulations rather than by its own mission. Moreover, by

the time it is clear that the program needs to be changed or abandoned, the donor is usually deceased and the terms for changing how the funds are spent may not be in place. If the endowment is large enough, lengthy and expensive court cases may result. · Managing an endowment is an additional piece of work for board and staff. This management time can become the tail that wags the dog, particularly if there are problems with the investments or disagreement about how to use the income. CONSIDERING AN ENDOWMENT OR RESERVE FUND It is obvious that only organizations with strong annual campaigns are really in a position to start endowments. When thinking of starting an endowment, organizations often focus on the money: how much to raise, how to raise it, whom to ask for it. But there are two critical questions that must be answered before even one dollar is invested in your endowment. Does Everyone in the Organization Agree That Your Group Should Exist Permanently? Most nonprofits involved in social change are formed with the idea that if their work is successful, they will put themselves out of business. The founders generally do not think of the group becoming permanent, and everyone may be surprised at how long it is taking to solve the problem the organization was created to address. Arts groups, independent schools, historic preservation societies, parks and wildlands conservation groups, and some social services are clearly permanent, with their work always needed or wanted. On the other hand, environmental, feminist, liberation, and advocacy groups, if they are successful, will cease to exist. Sometimes the most interesting part of the endowment process is discussion of this question at the beginning: Should we always be here? "Permanence" in terms of endowment has shades of meaning. It can take its traditional meaning of "always and forever" or it can take the meaning of "fifty years from now." But endowments do imply existing well past the lifetime of anyone in the group, and they require the group to imagine the day when people who are not yet born are sitting on the board of directors and working as staff. Will your group be needed then? What is the evidence of that need? It is important to make sure that everyone among board, staff, key volunteers, and donors agrees that permanence is a value. When people don't agree on that condition, the fundamental reason to have an endowment and the driving force of endowment fundraising are already in trouble. What Will Endowment Income Be Used For? Just as couples may have differing ideas about how and when to use savings, so may board and staff differ about using endowment income. Some will see the income stream as a relief from constant fundraising and will not expect the group's annual budget to grow substantially. Others will see the endowment income as paying for particular programs or doing things the group has not been able to do before.

13

Launching Major Campaigns

Once an organization has mastered the process of identifying prospects for major gifts, asking them for money, and developed a working major gifts program, it is ready to consider moving to a more formal major gifts campaign. The main differences between an ongoing major gifts program and a major gifts campaign are that a campaign is time-limited—it begins and ends on specific dates; the goal of the campaign is made public; and markers toward achieving the goal are announced frequently, as in thermometers showing how far the group has come toward its goal, announcements in the newsletter, and so on. Reaching or surpassing the goal in the time frame that is set becomes part of the excitement. Although a major gifts program has a goal that is part of the organization's overall fundraising plan, the program is in place all year and the goal is not necessarily public. You have a full fiscal year to reach the goal, and achieving it feels like no more of an accomplishment than the fact of meeting your budget. Because a major gifts campaign, on the other hand, is time-limited and public, you can use it to generate publicity about the overall needs of the organization. During the time of the major gifts campaign, a few volunteers devote themselves intensively to meeting a specific financial goal, giving amounts of time and effort to the campaign that would be difficult to maintain beyond a short commitment. A major gifts campaign requires nine steps, some of which are the same as for any major gifts program. The steps are listed below, then discussed in detail. 1. Set a goal 2. Prepare supporting materials 3. Identify and train solicitors 4. Identify prospects 5. Assign prospects and solicit gifts 6. Kick off the campaign with a special event (optional, though it can attract media attention and recognize donors) 7. Hold regular reporting meetings 8. Celebrate the end of a successful campaign with a special event (also optional, though it can attract media and recognize donors) 9. Thank donors, record gifts, and incorporate new *donors into ongoing fundraising efforts THE STEPS IN DETAIL Step 1: Set a Goal The first step in a major gifts campaign is to decide how long the campaign will last and how much money will be raised. For small organizations, a campaign of six to eight weeks is ideal because volunteers and overworked staff can maintain momentum and excitement for that much time fairly easily and a lot of money can be raised in this short period of time. To determine a fundraising goal, first calculate how many prospects could be asked in that length of time. Generally, a volunteer can ask about one to three people a week for six to eight weeks without undue strain. A committee of five volunteers, then, could ask between 40 and 120 people during an eight-week campaign. Assuming the usual 50 percent rate of success, your group would have from 20 to 60 new major donors after such a campaign. If you have a shortage of volunteers, you can ask each volunteer to solicit more people per week, but only volunteers with a lot of time and comfort with the process of asking will be able to do more than twelve asks in one month. Your better bet will be to lower the goal so that the major gifts campaign is something volunteers will want to do again, not something they gave their all to and burned out doing. Knowing how many gifts you can get, now plot how many gifts of specific amounts you will need in order to reach your goal, using the following method. Select the lowest amount that will be solicited in face-to-face meetings. Most groups choose $500 as the minimum request for which they will seek a meeting; others start in-person solicitations for gifts of $250. Rarely would it be worth the time to make face-to-face solicitations for less than $100. Next, determine what your largest gift will be, which is usually 10 percent of the total goal. With the largest and lowest gifts decided on, you can chart what size gifts you will need and how many of each to meet the goal.*

14

Understanding Capital Campaigns

———◆♡◆———

Acapital campaign is an intensive, time-limited effort to raise money for a project that presents a one-time need over and above the annual budget. Capital campaigns are traditionally used to finance buying, constructing, or refurbishing a building; more and more frequently, they are being used to begin an endowment. The financial goal of a capital campaign is often at least as large as the organization's annual budget and often many times larger. Most capital campaigns last two to three years; some go on as long as five years. Capital campaigns allow donors to pledge a large amount and take as many as five years (and for very large pledges, ten years) to pay it off. Donors are asked to give to the capital campaign in addition to their regular annual donations, and they are explicitly asked not to decrease their annual gift in order to make a capital gift. Capital gifts are usually so large that the donor cannot finance the gift from their income and must donate cash from savings or other assets (stocks, real estate, art). In understanding a capital campaign, it is helpful to review the fundraising context, first presented in Chapter Three, in which a capital campaign would be the strategy chosen. THE ORGANIZATION AND ITS FINANCIAL NEEDS Organizations have three types of financial needs: Annual Funding. The money they need every year. For most grassroots groups, raising this money consumes all their fundraising time. Capital Funding. From time to time, groups need something that they don't need every year. Items such as computers, a new phone system, or furniture; or maintenance, such as rewiring or installing carpeting are capital improvements. For these, additional money needs to be raised beyond a group's annual budget. For small capital needs, a group may just add money to its annual budget and raise it with an extra *appeal, or it may submit a proposal to a foundation or an appeal to a generous major donor. When the capital improvement involves buying, retrofitting, or renovating a building, the group usually needs to conduct some kind of campaign to raise the money from a number of sources. Endowment Funding. As discussed in Chapter Twenty-Two, organizations that think they will be needed forever, or at least as far into the future as they can project, will want to invest some of their money and use only the interest from the investment as part of their annual income. The principal that is set aside to be invested is usually referred to as an endowment. Donors can provide income for these various funding needs through a few different vehicles: Gifts of Income. The majority of people earn money every year from a job, investments, a pension, or some combination of these sources. About seven out of every ten people give some of their earned income away. These gifts generally provide for the annual needs of the organizations they donate to. In other words, some of my income as a donor becomes some of your income as an organization. Gifts of Assets. In addition to their income, many people have saved or inherited assets that are in various forms of investments—stock, real estate, bonds, art, insurance policies, and so on. A donor can also give these assets to an organization, which generally uses them for capital. In other words, I give some of my savings—or my capital—to increase the capital of an organization. Gifts from Estate. Everyone eventually dies, but as described in Chapter Twenty-One, they control what they own even in death through the terms of their will. Through their will, a trust, or other estate-planning mechanism, a donor can arrange for nonprofit organizations to receive some or all of their estate. These gifts are most often used for endowment. In other words, the last set of gifts I will give, which form my legacy, are used for the group to exist long after I am gone.Unless restricted by the donor, organizations can, of course, use gifts of assets and estate for their annual needs. In the case of very small gifts or when donors regularly give stock as their annual gift, this may be appropriate. But for the most part, using assets and estate gifts for annual purposes is unwise because these gifts will not recur. Similarly, but probably less obviously, using gifts made from a donor's income for capital or endowment purposes is also ill-advised. First, you don't want to raid your annual income for funds to pay for capital costs (a practice that, unfortunately, many groups do), and second, any amount that a person can afford to give from income they should be encouraged to give every year and not just for a onetime event such as a capital or endowment campaign. I hope that it goes without saying (but I will say it anyway, just in case) that if a person wishes to give a gift from their income to a capital or endowment effort, a group should not turn that gift away; they should accept it and thank the donor* *appropriately. When contemplating a capital campaign, many groups will say, "Our donors don't earn that kind of money." However, your donors' earnings are less important than their savings. I have seen groups mount successful capital campaigns with lead gifts from older donors living on fixed incomes who have some highly appreciated stock or a piece of property they are willing to give. Because the donor can deduct the fair-market value of their gift, they avoid the capital gains tax on that part of their savings, enabling them to make a much greater gift than they might have thought they could and at considerable tax savings. Keep in mind, then, that with a capital campaign you are not asking donors to make extra gifts from their income; you are asking them to go to a whole new level with your organization—giving assets and often paying their gift as a pledge over a period of several years. Some organizations elect to conduct a feasibility study before embarking on a capital campaign. Such a study will look at, among many other things, your donor's ability and willingness to access assets. (See Chapter Twenty-Six for more information on this.) BEST USE OF CAPITAL CAMPAIGNS Some grassroots groups have conducted what they called capital campaigns to buy new computers or to send staff to fundraising workshops, which meant their goal was $5,000 or less, their time frame was a few weeks, and people were simply asked to put in a few extra dollars. However, capital campaigns are best used to seek gifts of assets from a wide pool of people and institutions, not just to seek "something extra" from the annual incomes of current donors. Capital campaigns should be seeking people in your donor base who may own property or securities and who would not help you in this way every year, but might give you a big gift once in a while. For this to be your intention, your capital campaign goal needs to be at least $100,000. If you need to raise less than $100,000, consider structuring your campaign as a major gifts campaign as described in Chapter Twenty-Three and run the campaign for a short time during one year, or seek two or three foundation or corporate grants to meet the goal and don't run a campaign at all. Although your most loyal annual donors will also give to a capital campaign if they can, there are many other types of people who give to capital campaigns who are not regular annual donors. For example, three years ago a local attorney helped a small community organization in Alabama file a lawsuit against their city. The attorney admired the group's feistiness and their willingness to take risks. She was impressed that the sole staff person would work for a low salary and that the volunteers put in many hours at the organization beyond their own jobs elsewhere. She did not charge for her assistance with the lawsuit, and she donated $100 after it was over. Because she did not wish to become a regular donor to this group,* *she did not respond to their subsequent annual appeals. However, she did have lunch with the executive director from time to time, and she continued to provide legal advice when asked. She bought a table at their annual event for $1,000 for two years in a row, and she gave the group $2,000 when asked to help send a number of their constituents to a conference. When, a few years later, the organization decided to buy a building to house their organization, they asked her for a lead gift of $20,000. The work she had done pro bono on the lawsuit had been worth about that much, and the staff figured she still admired them. She did, and she admired their boldness in asking her. She gave $10,000 outright and pledged an additional $10,000 as a challenge to be met by other lawyers. Universities and private schools often have the experience of receiving a onetime gift to a capital campaign from an alumnus or alumna who had been a minimal donor prior to the campaign. Some people like the idea of contributing to something as substantial as a building. To ask donors to stretch their own giving and to seek donations outside of the immediate "donor family" means having a goal that implies stretching will be required to meet it. It must seem to a prospect—including a corporation, government agency, foundation, or religious institution that might not support your annual program work—that the organization cannot get this money simply by asking a few people or writing a single grant proposal. BEGINNING A CAPITAL CAMPAIGN A capital campaign begins when the organization has identified a large one-time need. The board of directors must fully concur with this need and must support the idea of conducting a capital campaign, which is a lot of extra work for everyone and may require an initial outlay of money to hire extra staff and develop materials. Key volunteers who are not on the board along with long-time major donors should also be consulted about doing a capital campaign. Everyone who is important to an organization should have an opportunity to voice his or her concerns and feel part of the decision. There are dozens of buildings in the United States that are underutilized because key people in the organization were divided about the idea of constructing a new building and the people opposed to the capital campaign were outvoted. The organization may have had a few donors or funders who paid for the building, but without a lot of community support, the building is more albatross than asset. Sometimes the organization has enough money for the building, but exhausts all its donors in the capital campaign and doesn't have the money to run all their programs or sometimes even to finish furnishing the building. So the building becomes underutilized. In other instances, campaigns have had to be called off halfway through the process because so many volunteers and donors had left the organization to protest doing the campaign in the first* *place. A capital campaign is a highly visible enterprise; it needs widespread support within the organization. Estimating Costs After all the parties have been consulted and there is general agreement on the need, a goal needs to be set. Similar to the understanding that in a fancy restaurant the eventual cost of the meal will be double the entree (with drinks, dessert, and tip) the true cost of a campaign is far more than the cost of the project itself. One group learned this fact the hard way. They needed larger office space and decided that buying a building would, in the long run, be less expensive than continually paying rent. They found a building that suited them priced at $250,000. The group launched their campaign for $250,000, forgetting that there would also be closing costs, insurance, furnishings, the cost of the campaign, and so on. In the end, the true cost of the building was $310,000. The organization spent two years climbing out of a $60,000 deficit caused by their lack of understanding the full financial implications of the building purchase. The following items need to be added in to the actual cost of buying or constructing a building or starting an endowment: Fundraising Materials. Materials to be used for the campaign include a case statement, brochures, pledge cards, background information for solicitors, pictures, architect's renderings, a special newsletter to capital campaign donors to keep them informed of progress, and a prospectus (see page 314). Cost of Staff Time. Someone has to handle pledges, write thank you notes, report to the board, work with the contractor, decide who has to approve paint color or carpet choices, know what to do when someone donates stocks, and handle emergencies. Record Keeping. A process needs to be set up to keep the campaign's income and expenses separate from the annual budget and to collect pledges (which may extend well past the end of the campaign). If you plan to use current staff to do that, then someone will have to do some of their work. In a multiyear campaign, it is unlikely that a group could get by without hiring extra staff. Office Extras. You may need to put in extra phone lines or buy more computers. If you hire staff, that person will need to sit somewhere, so you may need another desk and chair. For the Building Project Itself. Someone with expertise in this area will need to help you list costs related to the building, such as construction insurance, building permits, design costs, disaster preparedness, fire extinguishers, landscaping, plumbing, and wiring, and help you with how much to estimate for cost overruns or unforeseen delays. Furnishings for the Building. What are you going to bring from your current office and what else will you need? What will these items cost?*

Debt Service on a Bridge Loan. You will probably have to pay bills before pledges are fully paid, and you may have to borrow money to cover the gap between pledged income and received income. The interest on that debt needs to be factored into the goal of the campaign. Banks will lend money with pledges as collateral, but you have to pay interest on the loan. Additional Costs. Add 15 percent for people who pledge but cannot finish paying or decide not to pay. Add another 5 to 10 percent onto the grand total and you can feel reasonably safe that this will be the cost of the campaign. In any fundraising endeavor, but particularly in campaigns with big-ticket items such as buildings, follow the adage: Plan expenses high and income low. Preparing a Case Statement Once the need is established and the costs are known and provisionally approved by the board, the next step is to write up a case statement for the campaign. This case statement is separate from the organization's overall case statement, although certainly it borrows from it. The capital campaign case focuses solely on the goal of the campaign and shows how this goal will help the organization meet all its other goals. The case statement implies or overtly states that the work of the group will be greatly enhanced by the addition of whatever the campaign is proposing to achieve and will be significantly slowed down or impaired by the lack of whatever is being proposed. The final page of the case statement is the financial goal displayed as a gift range chart. The Gift Range Chart The pyramid that is constructed by a capital campaign gift range chart is much shorter and narrower than that of an annual major gifts campaign (see Chapter Eighteen). In a capital campaign, the lead gift equals between 15 and 20 percent of the total goal, and 80 percent of the money comes from about 10 percent of the donors. The gift range chart follows this pattern: One gift = 15 to 20 percent or more of the goal Two gifts = 10 percent each or more Four to five gifts = 5 percent each or more So, 50 percent to 70 percent of the goal will come from about seven or eight gifts.

15

Developing Endowment Campaigns

An endowment campaign has the same structure as an annual fund campaign, a major donor campaign, or a capital campaign in that it has a financial goal for which a gift range chart and time line have been developed to help the organization meet that goal. Many organizations conduct a feasibility study to determine what the goal of the campaign should be or even whether to commit to the campaign at all. (See Chapter Twenty-Six for a discussion of feasibility studies.) As with a capital campaign, the tasks for launching an endowment campaign include forming a committee of solicitors, compiling a list of prospects, and developing creative materials that describe the campaign and its benefits. Once these tasks have been done, the prospects are prioritized and solicitation begins. Unlike other types of campaigns, an endowment remains open for new gifts even after the campaign has ended. The gifts sought during the campaign are from donors who will give over the next few years; gifts through estates are not the focus of this campaign. For all the similarities of the steps, in each of them there are subtle and not-sosubtle differences between endowment campaigns and other kinds of campaigns. STEP 1: SET A GOAL To determine a goal for your endowment campaign, you need to decide how much interest income you want and what amount of principal will be likely to generate that amount of interest. A financial adviser will be able to help you with projections; these must also take into account whether you are investing only for income or for both income and growth. In addition, consider whether you want your endowment principal to keep pace with inflation, which will mean reinvesting some income back into the principal or investing at least some principal in growth stocks. Generally, an organization can safely assume that they can take the equivalent of

5 percent of the principal out every year and the principal will continue to grow. To generate $50,000 a year in interest income, then, will require an endowment of about $1 million; to generate $200,000 a year will require an endowment of $4,000,000. An endowment is not a quick fix to a cash flow problem! There are two ways to get to your goal: one is to conduct a campaign for that goal. If you need $1 million, your campaign goal is $1 million. However, if that sum seems out of your reach right now but you think you could get to, say, $250,000, you can conduct a campaign to "seed" your endowment fund. With this type of campaign, you raise a decent amount of money and do not draw anything out the account it until it gets to the initial goal you have set. Once the campaign is ended, you keep raising endowment funds as part of your fundraising work, but without the intensity of a campaign. Having some money raised will help donors feel more assured that their endowment gift is joining existing money. The problem with the "seeding" approach, however, is that too often the endowment levels off at the small amount raised by the campaign. The endowment principal is too much money for the organization to spend, but not enough to generate the kind of interest that will really help with the annual fundraising crunch. If you decide to seed an endowment with a campaign, then, be sure that you have a plan in place for having the endowment grow after the campaign is over. Sometimes groups just want "something to take the edge off"—the stiff drink approach to endowments. They want a pot of money that generates between $5,000 and $10,000 a year, so they only need between $100,000 and $250,000. An endowment campaign is not the best vehicle to raise this small amount of money. For any need of less than $25,000, an organization should consider increasing its annual fundraising goal, perhaps by diversifying to a new strategy or being more aggressive with current donors. Generally, it is not worth the effort of starting an actual endowment campaign if your goal is to raise less than $500,000. Of course, however much money you decide to raise in your campaign, you should always be seeking and accepting additional endowment gifts. But keep your endowment moving by setting a large enough goal to be meaningful.

STEP 2: CREATE THE GIFT RANGE CHART Once you have a goal, you need to create a gift range chart. A chart for a goal of $1 million is shown below. As with capital campaigns discussed in the previous chapter, an endowment campaign differs from an annual major donor campaign in that it seeks a lead gift that is generally 20 percent of the goal instead of 10 percent, and all the gifts are fairly large. The chart calls for one gift to equal 20 percent of the goal, two gifts to equal 10 percent of the goal, and three to five gifts to equal the next 10 percent of the goal. Six to eight donors, then, contribute 50 percent or more of the total goal.

STEP 3: CREATE THE TIMELINE The timeline for an endowment campaign is generally not less than two years and definitely not more than five years. The timeline for the campaign does not include all the discussion involved in deciding to do a campaign or the feasibility study, but it does include the preparation time in terms of prospect research and materials. It usually takes the best part of a year just to solicit the lead gifts (because many of the lead donors will have to be talked with several times) and to create appropriate materials, and it may take another year to solicit all the other gifts. Three years allows for the unforeseen to be dealt with and the maximum number of donors to be solicited. Five years is the outside maximum amount of time an organization can sustain interest and passion for a campaign while maintaining annual fundraising. Usually two to three years is the ideal amount of time to conduct a campaign. A fourth year can be used as a "wind-down" period, and pledges can be paid over five or more years even if the solicitation phase of the campaign is completed in two years. STEP 4: FORM A SOLICITATION TEAM Traditionally, endowments are funded by gifts from estates. This is why traditional endowments cannot be conducted as campaigns, because the receipt of the gift usually depends on the death of the donor as well as the time it takes to settle the estate (which can be years). Some groups have counted the unrealized value of bequests as part of their endowment campaign goal, but this is both foolish and unethical. Bequests can be changed any time before the donor's death, so even when a donor has promised you a bequest, it may not happen if the donor has a change of heart or circumstance. Only irrevocable—unable to be revoked—legacy gifts (such as trusts) can be counted toward a goal. In conducting an endowment campaign, organizations are asking donors for assets: gifts given during the donor's lifetime. (Because an endowment lasts forever, a gift from a donor's estate is welcome; many endowments are built mostly or entirely from estate gifts. However, a campaign format means that we seek gifts that are made in the donor's lifetime—in fact that are paid in the next few years.) Although gifts made from a donor's annual income are certainly welcome, they will never be as large as assets or estate gifts, because even the wealthiest donors reserve the bulk of their income for their own needs. In forming a committee, then, you are looking for people who are comfortable asking donors for assets; usually, these are people who have made an asset gift themselves. The people on the solicitation team include members of the board and people who have made large gifts to the endowment. Although this is the ideal committee makeup for any campaign, for an endowment it is imperative that those who are asking know what it feels like to decide to give a gift that they cannot give very often. The role of volunteers in these campaigns cannot be overstated. Staff *can ask, and they do, but even then a staff person will need to have made a endowment gift in addition to their annual gift. To form the solicitation team, first identify the people closest to the group who can make the largest gifts. A team consisting of a board member and a staff member asks each of these potential solicitors for their own gift, then asks them to be on the team. Some members of the solicitation team are usually identified during the discussion about whether to have an endowment. They are the ones who argue in favor of it and say that they will give to such a campaign. Conventional financial planning dictates that one should "never touch principal." Yet principal is what you are asking for. In a sense, you are asking people to transfer some of their "endowment" to your endowment. This is a process that requires thought, commitment, and careful consideration. All the solicitors must be people whom the donors trust to have gone through this process. Moreover, there is something very convincing when a person can say, "My husband and I have accumulated a nest egg of $100,000 over many years of saving. It is for our retirement and for emergencies. But the threat to reproductive rights (or environment, our children, or world peace) is bigger than our need for a nest egg. We want to make sure that Important Group is able to do their work and not have to struggle so with fundraising. So we are giving $10,000 to the endowment as our investment in our community's future."*

STEP 5: COMPILE AND ORGANIZE THE LIST OF PROSPECTS In all campaigns, the rule of "top down, inside out" is the way to organize your prospects. Ben Franklin, who was one of America's earliest and best fundraisers, advised, "Apply to all those whom you know will give something; next, to those whom you are uncertain whether they will give anything or not, and show them the list of those who have given; and lastly, do not neglect those who you are sure will give nothing, for in some of them you will be mistaken." Franklin's advice is what we mean by "inside out." Start with the people closest to the group. Those will be board members (if they are not the closest people to the organization, then reconsider doing an endowment campaign), other major donors, volunteers, former board members and volunteers (assuming no ill will accompanied their becoming "former"), staff, and so on. Then, start from the top of that list and work your way down. The first gift should be solicited from the person closest to the organization who can give the biggest gift. This may not be the biggest gift you need, but it should be the biggest one you can get right now. Sometimes it is hard to figure out which of the people who are closest you should approach first. Think through who on the list can give the biggest gifts. This exercise should narrow your list somewhat. Now think about who is most excited about the endowment. Remember there are going to be major donors who love your organization's work *but who are not going to support the endowment. There will be some who simply don't agree that a grassroots organization should have an endowment. There will be some who have given to other endowments only to see the endowment funds spent on annual needs by a careless board. And there willbe others who wish your endowment effort well but are only interested in funding more immediate needs. Finding donors who agree with all three premises of the case for an endowment—that the organization currently needs some financial stability, needs to exist indefinitely into the future, and is mature enough or sophisticated enough to handle this kind of money—and who also have the capacity to give is not simple. Use common sense in identifying these prospects. Think about what else you know about the people on your list. For example, a person giving $50 every quarter might be close to the group, but she is probably far from the biggest donor. However, if her $50 gifts are derived from income earned from investments, then she definitely goes to the top of the list because perhaps she would give you the asset that is yielding that $50 each quarter. Someone who gave you $1,000 that he won in the lottery, whose gift prior to that was $25, and who actually ekes out a living as an artist, is not going to be high on the list, but he may be an excellent solicitor because he actually gave an asset that he could have used himself. Many people will say that they have no idea what assets their donors have. If you really have no idea, then you are going to have to find out more about your donors before you begin asking them for gifts to your endowment. However, a general easy rule to follow in soliciting capital or endowment gifts is to ask for a gift that is ten times the amount of the donor's annual gift. You want to make it clear that this gift is in addition to their annual gift. You don't want your annual income to decline while you are doing the campaign. When you tell donors that you are asking everyone for the same thing—ten times their annual gift—people are not offended, even if the size of the gift is absolutely out of their range. The real risk you take in following this formula without other knowledge is that you would ask someone for too little. The final step in compiling a prospect list is to be sure you have enough prospects. A prospect for an endowment gift is someone who has demonstrated a commitment to your group, usually by giving over several years and often through other than just financial involvement; someone who has the money; and someone whom you know or you have access to. As with capital campaigns, you need about four times as many prospects as the number of gifts you seek because 50 percent of your prospects will say no and 50 percent of the group that says yes will give you less than what you ask for. In our $1 million gift range chart shown above, you would need about 348 prospects (87 × 4) to be certain that you could complete this goal. You don't need to have all* *the prospects right at the start, but you do need at least some of the prospects for the biggest gifts right from the beginning. You would be ill advised to launch a milliondollar endowment campaign with fewer than one hundred prospects for the gifts of $2,500 or more. Far worse than no endowment at all is an endowment campaign that sputters and moves slowly. The energy of the campaign is part of what makes it successful or not. A report that "Our campaign is going so well" makes people want to give. The news that "Our campaign is getting off to a slow start," or "We asked a bunch of people who said no" is not as appealing. STEP 6: SOLICIT THE GIFTS For a full description of the process of soliciting large gifts, please re-read Chapters Eighteen, Twenty-Three, and Twenty-Four on major gifts programs, major gift campaigns, and capital campaigns. The primary differences between major gifts or capital campaigns and endowment campaigns is in the case. A person being asked for a major gift needs to be convinced that there is a pressing, immediate need that your organization can meet and that this need must be addressed with, among other things, some very large gifts. A capital campaign makes the case that the pressing needs of the organization cannot be met adequately in the facility you are in or with the equipment you currently have or without some other large investment. The case for the endowment goes one step further, explaining that the organization needs stability currently and into the future. It tells the donor that his or her commitment to your current programs is so important that you hope they want to help make your work a permanent feature of your community. Even the most progressive person becomes a fiscal conservative when asked for capital or endowment gifts. They may well believe that your organization does wonderful things toward ending racism or providing creative learning opportunities for kids with disabilities or advocating for more just tax policies. But do these same donors believe you will be able to manage investing large amounts of money or be good at managing a building? Donors will have these questions, and organizations must be able to respond to them. When an organization wants to start an endowment, there will be an added question that no one can really answer: "What will happen when everyone who is currently involved in this organization is gone?" Taking seriously the right (and indeed, the obligation) of donors to raise these questions and doubts and preparing thoughtful and reasonable answers are the marks of organizations ready for capital and endowment projects.*

16

Conducting Feasibility Studies

A feasibility study is a survey of people whose agreement and support you would need in order to succeed at a particular project. Usually, prospective donors, board members, community leaders, and program officers at foundations and corporations who might be approached to contribute to a project are asked to state anonymously what they think about your capital or endowment project and what level of support they or their organization might provide. Generally, the survey is done in two or three parts: a written survey sent to all the prospects who will be asked for major gifts, a phone survey to a smaller number of donors who will probably be asked for lead gifts, and an optional handful of in-person interviews or a focus group with key leaders. WHO CONDUCTS THE FEASIBILITY STUDY Most organizations hire a consultant to carry out their feasibility study. The reason for this is straightforward: in order for the prospects to feel that they can be as honest and candid as they want, their answers have to be truly anonymous. Maximum anonymity is ensured when they are asked by a consultant whom they don't know to fill out a form sent by mail that does not call for them to include their name and address and that they return to the consultant, not the organization. Although some people might be willing to say whatever they want to say to anyone, human nature is such that to spare someone's feelings or to avoid a confrontation, many people will not be as direct if they know that what they say is going to get back to someone they know. The written survey consists mostly of structured questions presented in a multiple-choice format so that the results can be easily tabulated. A few openended questions can also be included to get more information about anything else the prospect might want to add about his or her confidence in the leadership of the organization or the program directions it is taking. Once those results are in, the consultant or other person doing the feasibility study looks for any *pattern of response or issues that need to be clarified. The results of the written survey form the basis of the questions in the phone survey. On the phone, the surveyor can probe a little more, record anecdotes and examples, and even query respondents about whether they agree or disagree with some of the opinions or findings that came from the written survey. Many studies don't include in-person interviews. They are helpful if there is a need to clarify the case or probe further about any anomalies found in the phone or written surveys, but otherwise you might have enough information to go on without them. A feasibility study is complicated and time consuming to conduct, which makes it expensive. The least-expensive study conducted by a professional will likely cost at least $5,000; many studies run as high as $25,000. The size of the income that can be expected from the campaign resulting from the feasibility study will not correlate directly to the cost of the study, because a campaign with a low goal will not necessarily involve fewer surveys or fewer phone calls. Because of the costs involved, these studies are usually reserved for large campaigns. WHETHER TO DO A STUDY There is no need to do a feasibility study in the following situations: · If you intend to do the campaign no matter what the study shows. I have known half a dozen organizations that spent money on a study only to conclude that the results showing lack of support were wrong. They proceeded with their campaigns—some succeeded and some failed. · If you are going to use the study simply to find out whether or not you can make your goal. You will discover easily enough whether you can raise the amount of money you need by asking for lead gifts from qualified prospects before the campaign is announced publicly. If they all say no or give much lower gifts than you needed, don't announce your campaign, and go back to the drawing board.· If your goal is less than $2 million, the cost of a full-scale study is not justified. You can decide to do only a written survey or a limited phone survey if you have some specific questions, but what you really want is to go to the lead prospects and see what they say. You will need to do a study under the following circumstances: · The key leadership in your organization has a mixed reputation. I conducted a study for a capital campaign for an organization whose executive director had been there thirteen years. She was well liked, but as one key prospect said, "The organization has gotten too big for her and neither she nor her board can handle the responsibility of a building." The study showed that unless the group made significant changes in staffing, such as hiring an associate director who could handle a lot of the administrative and human resource issues the executive director was not good at, few were likely to contribute. · Your building project may be controversial in some way. A proposed homeless shelter discovered that they would face major neighborhood* *opposition if they expanded in the way they envisioned. By slowing the process down, they were able to address neighborhood concerns with public education programs. Once that was done, the campaign proceeded successfully. · You want to raise more than $2 million and you have never raised that amount of money before. · You want to know exactly what the capacity of the people closest to the organization is before you ask them. The results of your study will not show you what any individual donor can give, but you will learn whether there are people in your sphere who have the capacity and willingness to give large amounts. You will need to figure out who those people are. A feasibility study gives you an added measure of assurance and will help you define and counter big problems. When raising large amounts of money, a feasibility study will allow you to discover the capacity of your donors in a way that would otherwise be difficult, given our society's strong taboo about talking about how much money a person actually has. In my experience, grassroots organizations that are able to raise the first third of their goal from five to ten people will be able to raise the rest of the money to get to their goal. I advise groups to use that guideline as the most reliable indicator of whether their campaign will succeed. If you want more assurance without having to buy a feasibility study, you can talk to the people who would have to take the lead for your campaign to succeed. Tell them about the possibility of the campaign and ask what they think about it. Tell them you are "testing the waters," or "getting feedback on this idea." Make the conversation very casual, but pay close attention to what they say. WHAT FEASIBILITY STUDIES TELL YOU Feasibility studies often predict that a campaign will bring in a lower amount than it actually raises in the end. Many consultants prefer to underestimate the amount that can be raised, but the main reason campaigns exceed their goals is that it is impossible to factor in the effect of the excitement generated by the campaign on the prospects. It is one thing for a prospect to talk on the phone about what they might, theoretically, do for a campaign should it be launched, but quite another for them to be asked in person to give to a campaign by someone they admire. On the phone, a person is sober and serious and not wanting to mislead the questioner. They name an amount that is perhaps a stretch for them but that they feel confident they would be able to pay. Later, during the real campaign, when a friend or colleague comes with a staff person to ask for their gift, they are likely to become excited by the enthusiasm of the askers, and end up giving more than they told the interviewer they might during the phone survey. Perhaps on the phone a prospect said they would be unlikely to give, but faced with the reality of the campaign they may not want to be left out. Their objections, which seemed so big during the phone call, can fade in the light of the campaign. This* *does not mean you should add on a few hundred thousand to whatever the study suggests you can raise, but it does mean that you can be confident that a well-done study will present an amount that is at or below what you can really bring in. ACHIEVING SUCCESS Of course, there is no assurance that any plan will succeed. But you have a better chance of succeeding if you have a plan than if you don't. Moreover, evaluating your success will be easier if you have a plan—in fact a plan is what makes evaluation possible.*

Another requirement for success is to make sure your board of directors is on board. If a board of directors does not want to work on the campaign, the campaign is going to go nowhere. People look to the board for leadership. Your board may well be made up of people who cannot make big gifts to a capital or endowment campaign. That's fine. But they need to make some gift, and they need to be involved in planning the campaign. The best way to know if you are going to succeed is to take the time to plan properly, as discussed in the chapters on capital and endowment campaigns, then implement the quiet phase of your plan. The requests made during the quiet phase give you the most accurate information with the least amount of public risk.

17

Managing Your Information

Amajor part of fundraising is information—about people, about sources of money, about timing, about strategies. But fundraising is not just knowing things. The creativity to make fundraising successful is in putting together what you know: asking the right person at the right time for the right amount; scheduling the right event and inviting the people most likely to be interested in attending; using volunteers to the best of their abilities. In order to use all the information available in the most effective ways, a fundraiser must know how to manage the information that is constantly coming in. Too often what one finds in the office of fundraising staff are piles of papers on the floor and windowsill interspersed with unlabelled CDs and multiple foundation guides. Desks are strewn with notes, Post-its are stuck all around the computer monitor, and a telephone is perched precariously atop the overflowing in-basket. The staff 's e-mail inbox will contain hundreds of e-newsletters and messages from the many listservs they subscribe to. Too often we mistake the message that such an office sends—the inability to get and stay organized—with being overworked. Since having too much work is often a major component of many fundraisers' lives, one compounds the other. A fundraiser confided to me recently that she was secretly relieved when her office flooded and her papers and hard drive were destroyed. Now she had an excuse for not getting work done she wouldn't have gotten to anyway. What has been called for the past twenty-five years the "information age" is really information glut. In addition to the traditional books and magazines about fundraising, new Web sites, listservs, e-newsletters, and computer programs pop up daily, ostensibly to help you gather and sort information in ways you never thought of. Dozens of toll-free numbers provide more information or technical support for your must-have new module on your database. There is more to know about everything than any human can process;

moreover there are mountains of misinformation. People in fundraising must always be clear about what they need to do and what they don't. This chapter will help you deal with the overload of information. INFORMATION YOU NEED FOR FUNDRAISING In order to know what to keep, what to throw out, what to delete, what to order, and what to file, you must make a list of priorities about your job. What information do you need to be on top of, what do you need to have access to from time to time, and what doesn't matter at all? While the answers to these questions will vary from person to person, most fundraisers must keep track of the following information that is the most important to their work: · Information pertaining to current donors · Information pertaining to prospects · Information about the organization that will be used to get more donors and prospects · Reference materials and records about past fundraising activities Any papers that come across your desk or any e-mail that pops up on your screen that does not pertain to the categories listed here needs to be deleted, recycled, or at least put out of sight. Among other items that will get tossed are newsletters from other groups unrelated to your group, advertisements for seminars and classes, catalogues, annual reports of foundations your group will not be applying to, old annual reports of prospective foundations, old to-do lists, and reports on all causes unrelated to your group. Similarly, delete any files that are not related to current or prospective donors, past donors, or past fundraising efforts, as well as ancillary information about any of those items. In your physical filing cabinet, use the bottom file drawer for reference material about your group. Put in that drawer one copy each of your past newsletters, proposals funded, evaluations of direct mail appeals, reports on special events, board minutes and reports, and financial statements. Every piece of paper and every byte in your computer should be held up to this test: Will this item help me get money from someone? If yes, who and how? Then put it in the appropriate place: the prospect's file or the reference drawer. If the answer for any piece of paper or computer document is no, throw it out or delete it or forward it to another staff person whose work it will help. KEEPING TRACK Once you learn a few simple rules about what to keep and what to save, keeping track of information will actually not be that difficult. First, review the basics: What is your job? What do you have to know? What would people reasonably expect you to be able to lay your hands on quickly? Even if you are the only paid staff person, you still have a limit to your job. These are the types of information you must have and have easy access to: · Records of official meetings of the organization and reports offered to the board, the public, or the IRS about the organization. Keep one (at most two) copies of board minutes, audits, 990s, newsletters, direct mail appeals, annual reports, and so on. · Records on the donors: their names, addresses, and gift history, as well as information that would help you or someone else ask them for more money or for some other type of involvement. Most of this information is kept virtually in a database; it must be backed up every day on either a flash drive or backup disk. Once a week a copy of that back-up must be taken out of your office. There are other items you probably should have if you are a one-person shop— you decide. But do you really need copies of newsletters from organizations you are not interested in? Dozens of samples of invitations? (Pick the best ten and throw the rest away.) The latest reports from the most prolific think tanks on every subject from ozone depletion to police brutality, from campaign reform to the role of women in rural Hindu communities? No. What is your organization? You will be kept busy enough keeping up with what pertains to you. Having set priorities on the kinds of information you need—and limit yourself to five priorities at the most—sort all your papers into those categories and throw away anything that doesn't fall into them. Especially throw away the volumes of information you now keep that you feel you "should" read: the stuff that you bring home but never quite get to, the stuff you downloaded to read in the airport but always manage to ignore in favor of something else you have found. If you feel that you "should" read it, you won't. Lighten up. It's all right not to read everything; it's even all right not to read most things. The final guideline about what to throw out is that if you haven't looked at it in six months and it is not needed for the IRS or as an archive copy, throw it out. YOUR FILING SYSTEM Next, think through your filing system for both your paper and your computer files. Create broad categories, then file within those categories. Categories might include board, donors, prospects, foundations, finances, programs, personnel, and publications. You may want to keep some of these items in files for each year. Within some of those categories you may want subcategories. For example, the board section might have the following subcategories: board members—current, past, potential; board reimbursements; board minutes; staff reports to the board. The files in some of these categories will be arranged alphabetically, in others chronologically. For example, board minutes and reports to the board should be filed chronologically. To test your filing system, ask a friend or another staff person to come into your office and start naming things for you to find. It should not take you more than two minutes to lay your hands on or bring up on your computer any piece of information you are in charge of. If you can't do that, reassess your system. Once your system passes this test, see how well it works for someone else. Suppose you were hit by a train—how obvious is your information set-up? If it takes someone else more than five minutes to figure out where something is, your system is too mysterious. Many otherwise neat people have sloppy virtual files, so give this problem extra attention. I know, because I am one of these people. Virtual files fool you because you don't often notice how much room these are taking up—the "clutter" is invisible, so it is easy to let the information on hard drives get out of control. I, who rarely handle a piece of paper more than once, will spend an hour scrolling through my files with the intensity of a mad scientist—did I save it under "November" because it happened in November, or under "Special Events-Ideas-Fall Plans" or in "Docs-Fundraising-Special Events-November"? Why would I even have a filing system like that? The same standards apply to computer files as to paper files: Will you need it again? How can you name the file and the subfile so their contents are obvious?

As you save documents on your computer, think about what you name them. There are people who name their files after the day of the week or even an abbreviation of something in the file, but all of this makes the files obscure even to the one who named them. Again, apply the standard, "If I were hit by a train, could someone else find this?" Give it a name that makes some sense. Spend time clearing out your computer files. STICKING WITH IT To help you stay on top of your papers and computer files once you get organized, post a 3 × 5 card with the one, two, or three things that will most help you stay focused on what to keep. One person has this on his card: Is it a donor? Is it a prospect? Could it lead to a donor or a prospect? Another has this: When in doubt, throw it out. After all, what is the worst thing that can happen? Another's says: If this were my last day at work and I was sorting through my stuff, would I give it to the person succeeding me? In our business, information is like food: we eat it, we serve it to others, we save it for a few days, but we don't keep it permanently. It is useful for what it does for us, but is not really useful beyond being converted to energy, enjoyment, or in this case, donors. Seeing information in that light will let you be in control of it so that you can use it to do your work.

18

Managing Your Time

Effective time management often marks the difference between a good fundraiser and someone who is never going to make it in this field. First, remember that the fundraising job is never done and you are never caught up on your work. Also, Murphy's Law says that expenses rise to meet income. The more successful the fundraising plans are, the more plans the organization will make to spend that money. Consequently, no amount of money raised is ever enough. Fundraising staff (paid and unpaid) must set their own limits because no matter how supportive the organization may be of your work, it is still relentless in its need for more money. Here are some guidelines for using your time to best advantage. GUIDELINES There are certain tasks that must be completed either every day or every week. Every Day Reserve Time When You Cannot Be Interrupted. For one (and sometimes two or three) hours each day, let someone else or your voice mail answer the phone. Do not talk to other staff, and do not reply to e-mail. Use that time for research and writing. Write To-Do Lists at the End of Each Day. Spend fifteen to thirty minutes at the end of the day writing up a to-do list for the next day. At the beginning of the day, review your to-do list. Unless something comes up that really can't wait, do only those tasks already on your to-do list. Put new things on tomorrow's list. Make Sure Thank You Notes Are Getting Written. Ideally, a board member or volunteer is coming into the office to write thank you notes on a regular basis, or the executive director is adding a personal note to a thank you generated by your database program. You must stay on top of this process. Update Your Database. This task often happens when you are entering the information that will enable you to generate a thank you note, but don't get behind on it. Every Week Review Your Fundraising Plan for the Month. Go over your plan to make sure you are on target. Don't put off tasks such as getting a letter to the printer, calling a foundation, setting up meetings of the major gifts committee or the special events committee. Do these tasks on time. Watch for Time Sinks. How many times have we looked up at a clock and in total disbelief said, "How could it be four o'clock?" or "Where did the day go?" Sometimes this is a sign that we have been absorbed in important work, but sometimes it is a sign that we have used up our time doing a lot of stuff that seemed important but wasn't, or that is important but could have been handled in a fraction of the time. Here are the most common time sinks: The Telephone. Limit the length of your calls by standing up while you are on the phone. If you know the telephone is a big temptation for you, move it off your desk so that you actually have to move to answer it or to make a phone call. Because you know that for most of the calls you make you will get voice mail, spend a few seconds before you call thinking about the exact message you are going to leave. We all hate to get rambling or disjointed messages, yet many of us leave them. This wastes our time and the time of the person we are phoning. While friendliness and warmth are wonderful, limit yourself to one expression of either of these: "Hope your day is going well" does not have to be followed by, "And I hope your weekend was fabulous," or "And I hope you are feeling good and having time to enjoy this wonderful weather." Ditto with "OK, take care. Look forward to talking with you. Great to hear your voice." Pick one of those, preferably a short one. E-Mail. What could have been a great time-saving device has become the greatest time sink ever. Get off of listervs that you don't find useful or that are unrelated to your work. Delete without reading anything that has been forwarded to you that you know is simply a list of jokes or a petition. Don't feel obligated to answer every e-mail, particularly if you get e-mail from people who are not and are never going to be important to your group or who would never have paid the money to call you. Limit yourself to looking at your e-mail three or four times a day. Check it first thing in the morning, at the end of the morning, in midafternoon, and right before you go home. Don't check your work e-mail in the evening. Chatty Coworkers. Learn to sort out what kinds of conversations are important for maintaining morale and showing interest in other people, and what conversations simply occur because you or your coworker is procrastinating getting work done. Schedule social time with coworkers you like so that you will not have to steal time away from work. When you spend time talking with someone when you know you should be working, you are neither really enjoying the conversation nor, obviously, getting your work done. People Who Drop By. If someone comes by whom you don't need to talk with and you don't have time to talk, try the following tactics: tell them that you will call them later, or set a lunch date right then, or stand up and remain standing while talking to them (they will not sit down if you are standing). Another tactic is, at a moment when you are the one speaking, look at your watch or your calendar. This will remind your visitor of time without you being rude. You never need to act hurried or rushed with spontaneous visitors so long as you don't get panicked about how you are going to get rid of them. CALENDARS AND ACTION PLANS Understanding that information is time-related is integral to running an efficient office. Once you have organized your office, paper, computer files, and desk in a way that allows you easy and quick access to the information you need and provides a sensible system that someone else can follow, assign a time by which you will have used or acted on the information you are keeping track of so effectively. There are two principal methods: calendars and action plans. Calendars Buy or make the following three calendars or use the calendar function in your computer or on your PDA: · A "Year-at-a-Glance" wall calendar. This calendar shows all twelve months at once, with boxes for each day within each month.

· A "Month-at-a-Glance" calendar. Some people get these calendars as desktop blotters. You can also buy a smaller, desktop calendar from a worthy group so you have uplifting stories or fabulous nature photos to look at. Just be sure that the box for each day has enough room to write a few lines. · An appointment calendar to carry with you in your purse or briefcase. This is a simple daily calendar with all the days of the year laid out two or so to a page. You can get all of these functions on your PDA and then sync them with your computer, which provides a useful back-up system. Don't, however, feel you must go to an electronic system to be efficient. What is best is what works best for you and what you can use most easily. Although you can certainly invest lots of money in fancy calendar systems or calendar functions that allow you to record your expenses, birthday reminders, car mileage, meeting notes, priority to-do lists, meeting agenda items, tax information, and the like, I have yet to meet anyone who actually used all those systems. Further (and this is not a judgment of these systems, simply an observation of people who use them), in my experience, the fancier and more expensive the system, the less reliable the person. I always know when someone pulls out the ten-pound calendar with multicolored tabs or turns on their super slimline state-of-the art PDA and begins pecking at it, that whatever they just said they would do will probably never happen. On the other hand, when someone takes the free calendar they got from their insurance agent or an inexpensive one bought at an office supply store and writes what they have committed to on the day the commitment is to be fulfilled, I am reasonably certain it will get done. In terms of calendars, then, the simpler the system, the more workable it is likely to be. Now take your "Year-at-a-Glance" calendar and cross out the

following days: · Major holidays and one or two days before and after those holidays · Your vacation · Your birthday (don't work on your birthday) · The day (or two, if you wish) after any work meeting or conference that you know will be grueling or for which you have to travel a long distance What you have left is close to the true number of days you could get work done. Now put a large dot on the dates of board meetings, the annual meeting, special events, proposal deadlines, newsletter deadlines, and any other meetings or deadlines that you can anticipate. With a marker, draw a line from each deadline back as many days as you think it will take you to prepare for it; if work will be generated by the event, extend your line for one or two days after the event. Whatever work days don't have lines, dots, or crossouts are days you can do the rest of your work. You now have a clear visual picture that allows you to assess quickly, "Can I take on this commitment?""Does it make sense for me to attend this conference when I will be exhausted from our annual retreat?""Should we conduct our major donor campaign during our audit?" Remember also that some of the days of the year will be used up by illness (yours, your partner's, your children's, and so on), by goofing off or not working efficiently, and by work emergencies that take precedence. Now take your "Month-at-a-Glance" desk calendar or your PDA task function and note the major task areas that have to be taken care of each day in order to keep on schedule, such as thank you notes, the tasks related to a special event, newsletter production, and so on. This calendar does not take the place of a to-do list. However, most people do not keep the relationship of their to-do list and their calendar clear enough. For example, someone calls you and asks for an appointment. You look at your appointment calendar and seeing a clear day, make the appointment, only to realize later that the day was kept clear because of the approaching deadlines covered by the to-do list. Whenever possible, set your meetings, appointments, lunch dates, and so on by referring to your yearly or monthly calendar. A day does not stand alone. Do you really want to have a 7 A.M. breakfast meeting with a major donor the morning after a board meeting that will run until 10 P.M.? Use the daily calendar that you carry with you for tracking current appointments, keeping addresses and phone numbers, making future meetings and appointments when you are not in your office, jotting notes from meetings, and so on. However, every two or three days (some people do this at the end of every day), move all relevant information from your daily calendar onto your to-do list or onto your hard drive. Note in your daily calendar the deadlines and days that are filled with writing or preparation, including all that you have already noted on your yearly calendar. Finally, make appointments with yourself. My friend Bill, who has a hard time saying no to anything, assigns meeting times to HH in his calendar. Then, when someone trying to set up a meeting with him leans over to peer at Bill's calendar and says, "Bill, looks like you have an open afternoon," Bill will have protected a hard day of work, even though it involves no appointments, with a long appointment with HH (HH stands for "ha-ha"). These fake appointments jar him into not saying yes. He can say, "I have a meeting," which for him, as for most people, is easier than saying, "I have to write the campaign brochure." It also spares him the frustration of having to respond when someone says, "This will only take twenty minutes—it will be good for you to have a break from your writing." Here are some things to avoid in using calendars and scheduling your time: Avoid Having a Home Calendar and a Work Calendar. People who maintain two calendars (one for work and one for social appointments) almost always miss their Monday morning appointments (because they don't have their work calendar with them) and are constantly trying to recall whether they can make an evening meeting on Thursday, because they think that's the night of their daughter's soccer match—or is that Wednesday? Your daily calendar shows your whole day, from home to work and back home. Put your important home-life appointments and activities in your single daily calendar. Avoid Bemoaning Your Busy Life. When you say to yourself or others, "I am so busy," or "I don't know how I'll get everything done," you tend to set up a selffulfilling prophesy. Further, comments such as these don't accomplish anything except to use up time. Most people are busy and few people get everything done. Tell yourself instead, "I can get this done. I have enough time." Skip Unnecessary Meetings or Conferences. Conferences, trainings, Webinars, workshops, and seminars are the order of the day. They are both expensive and time consuming and rarely worth either the time or expense. Choose the events where you will really learn something or see people you truly want to see. Then go and be there. Too often we decide to attend a conference half-heartedly and spend most of the time during the plenaries and workshops making notes or to-do lists for when we get back, sending text messages, or slipping out to answer our cell phone. If you choose to attend a conference or seminar, be there. Do not answer your cell phone during the sessions and do not call your office unless absolutely necessary.

Avoid Scheduling Too Many Meetings. Although we have work to do in meetings and admittedly, a certain amount of the work we do at meetings is socializing and building camaraderie, many meetings are not essential, and almost every meeting lasts too long. Question every meeting: Is this meeting necessary? If it is, do I need to be there? Can I be there for part of it and not all of it? If you have any say in the meeting, make sure there is an agenda with *times beside each item. People tend to talk for the amount of time that is listed. People can negotiate the need for extra time as it comes up. Action Plans One of the difficult things about working with individual donors is that this work has no externally determined deadlines, so you have to create your own. Once you have your calendars set up, you are ready for the next step in organizing your fundraising office: creating action plans. Whenever you work with a donor or a prospect, make a note in their record of what you intend to do next. This is called your "action plan" or more simply, the "next step." This information should be recorded in a separate field under their name in your database. An action plan is brief, such as, "Invite to Marian's house party," or "Call with outcome of organizing effort in Roane County," or "Send report on toxic waste dumping as soon as available." Then add a date by which you plan to take the action. Put this date in your calendar. Note the donor's last name or some identifying phrase that will remind you to check what you were going to do on that date. Contact-management software is very helpful for keeping up with these plans, but the built-in calendar and task function in most PDAs also do a great job, and simple paper and pen have worked well for decades. Find a system that works for you and use it. If you are systematic about your donors, for each major donor or major donor prospect you will have a date on which you are going to do something to move the process of building their relationship with the organization along. By spreading these dates out over the year, you can give more personal attention to donors and not get jammed with unrelated donor meetings during a campaign or at the end of the year. If you have thousands of donors, you will obviously have to decide which ones you want to work with personally, but the action plan concept can be used for group activity also, such as, "Oct. 1: All $50–$249 donors receive news alert mail appeal. A fundraiser's job is often compared to that of the circus performer who balances plates on sticks by keeping the plates twirling and runs from stick to stick to keep the spinning going. If she misses, a plate falls and may break. The calendar is the stick, and the action plans are the plates. This is how you keep your plates spinning and not falling. The overall idea is to have as little to remember as possible. You shouldn't have things in your memory that you could write down or enter in your computer. This system frees you to use your mind to be creative or to learn new details about new people and write those down later. The wide variety of tasks involved in fundraising are both exciting and one of the many difficulties of the job. You can minimize some of the difficulties by relatively simple procedures to keep your office running efficiently. A calendar and action plan system allows you to use the information you accumulate to raise maximum dollars for your organization.*

19
Keeping Records

Accurate, up-to-date, and thorough records that are easy to access are the most basic necessity for an ongoing fundraising program. Without such records, you have little capability to ask donors for more money, target projects to specific donor interests, track response to appeals, set goals, evaluate your progress against your plan, or any of the other requirements for maintaining and increasing your base of individual donors. Obviously, the most important thing to keep track of is information about your donors. The vast majority of even the tiniest organizations do this on a computer database. If you use a paper system, you still need to keep good records; most of this information will be the same for a paper system as for a computerized one. (At the risk of revealing myself to be a Luddite, I need to say that a paper system that works is preferable to a database that doesn't. People raised billions of dollars before there were even memory typewriters, let alone computers. However, a database that works well for you gives you a lot more options than any paper system and allows you to sort information in many useful ways, so I recommend getting one if you don't have one now.) Your database needs to be able to do at least the following five functions: · Hold a lot of names (preferably an infinite number) · Hold a lot of information in many fields about each name · Sort fields quickly and easily · Produce reports by compiling information (such as total number of gifts from the summer appeal, amount pledged versus amount received, difference in direct mail costs and income between this year and last year) · Merge with a word processing program for individualized letters and format labels of different sizes for mailings PURCHASING A DATABASE PROGRAM Although some off-the-shelf database programs can be customized to meet all of the requirements listed here and more, I strongly recommend getting a program designed for fundraising. All computer programs will have bugs that have to be fixed, and all people using computer programs will run up against the limitations of their own ability to understand a function and the inability of the manual to explain it. When you purchase a program designed for fundraising, there should be a technical support person you can call. If you have a customized database program, on the other hand, you have to hope that the person who customized it is available. Just in the last year, people have told me the following sad stories about using their customized database programs: "We can't get that database to do a mail merge for our major donor campaign and John, who designed it, is in Nepal for six months." "The database has freaked out! It won't sort anything and it freezes every five minutes. Mary, who customized it for us, is mad at us and won't help." "Fred, the guy who put this program together, decided that we need all new computers and refuses to fix this until we agree to buy them. Meanwhile, it seems to have lost all current information. I know it's in there, but I can't figure out how to restore it."

20

Managing Volunteers

On the other hand, I also see grassroots organizations that have twenty, thirty, and even one hundred regular volunteers. They have volunteers who have full-time jobs, children, and other volunteer commitments. They have volunteers who are on welfare, who are single parents, who travel half of the time for work, who are elderly and not able to come to meetings at night, and so on. In other words, we can still recruit and keep volunteers. What we need to do is focus on how, rather than how hard it is, to have a successful volunteer program. There are many fine books on volunteering; some are listed in Resource E and will be helpful for you to consult. Put briefly, there are five things you need to know to get volunteers productively involved in fundraising. Take the Time Necessary to Orient Volunteers to Your Fundraising Program. A two-hour in-service program in which you go over your budget, your fundraising goals, and your progress to date will set a good example of transparency and allow people to ask any questions they have or voice concerns. Such an in-service meeting can also set the context in which your fundraising plan is developed, as described in Chapter One, including where money comes from, how many nonprofits there are, who gives money away, and so on. Use this in-service especially to focus on your case statement; have volunteers practice describing your organization to each other and answering questions about it. Volunteers need to feel "in the know" and they need to feel competent with regard to describing mission, goals, and objectives of the organization. We often think a volunteer is unwilling to ask for money when in fact he or she may feel insecure about discussing the organization. I have often had volunteers say, "I didn't ask for the money because I thought I might do more harm than good in trying to explain what the organization is doing." Help Each Volunteer Choose the Fundraising Strategies They Will Feel Most Comfortable Doing. In this way, you play to volunteers' strengths. In their book, *The Accidental Fundraiser*, Stephanie Roth and Mimi Ho describe three broad categories of activities that volunteers will prefer, depending on their personality and confidence. First, there are those who prefer to raise money by entertaining. They happily host house parties and they are good at organizing other special events. They know how to make people feel welcomed, and they are good at thinking through what would be fun or interesting for a group of people. These volunteers often like to work in groups; they are the one you will find on special event committees. The second type are those volunteers who prefer to sell things: these volunteers are good at selling products or events. They are excellent people to staff a booth selling T-shirts, mugs, books, and so on that your organization produces or distributes. They will sell products to friends, neighbors, and family, and they can be relied on to sell tickets to events. However, they are less willing to ask for money directly, which brings us to the third, and smallest group. These are the people who prefer direct asking to doing other fundraising tasks. People in this group are likely to have a little more experience with fundraising; they know that if you ask enough people you will get the money you need. Many of these people are or have been in sales or real estate and have overcome their own psychological barriers to asking. Some of them come from countries where taboos about money are not as strong as in the United States. Both the sellers and the direct askers have stopped taking rejection personally. Of course, some people are good at all three approaches, whereas a minority of volunteers are not comfortable with any strategy that requires talking to people about money. This latter group can be put to work writing thank you notes, entering names and addresses into a database, researching foundation funders—anything that you need in fundraising that is not people oriented.

To create a list of tasks such volunteers can do is simple. With each task you begin each day, think to yourself, "Could a reasonable, intelligent person accomplish this task with a minimal amount of training?" If the answer is yes, ask yourself why you are doing it. Paid staff should as much as possible focus on doing things that an organization really could not expect a volunteer to do. Tasks that require technical knowledge, that are tremendously time consuming, or that involve a lot of sequencing should take up the bulk of a staff person's time. Remember That Good Enough Is Good Enough. Staff-volunteer tension can come about because the staff person wants the job done perfectly according to their own definition of perfect. For example, in a small nonprofit, two volunteers took on the task of writing and sending the e-newsletter, scheduled to go out on the third Thursday of each month. Over six months, three newsletters went out on time and three went out two days late. Most of the newsletters had a few typos. These lapses *were too much for the staff person, and she took the job back from the volunteers. Obviously, if the volunteers had usually been a week late with the newsletter and if it were riddled with typos, her action would be justified. But these volunteers were for the most part both reliable and thorough. Far too often in dealing with volunteers, the best becomes the enemy of the good. Show Genuine and Frequent Appreciation. Remember Cesar Chavez's dictum for organizing: "People are far more appreciative of what they do for you than of what you do for them." Thank them often. Thank you notes, thank you calls, and brief mentions at meetings go a long way. Flowers, plaques, and ribbons are fine, but they are not as important as the occasional grateful word. Give Volunteers Time Off. People need time off for good behavior. Many volunteer fundraisers have found that their reward for doing their work is more work. "Ruby, you did such a great job with the auction. You are a natural! Once you catch your breath, do you think you could chair the membership drive?" Such a comment is a sure way to guarantee that Ruby will run, not walk, away from your organization as soon as she can. Make sure that, unless the volunteer insists otherwise, volunteers have at least two or three months between intense fundraising activities and that they are encouraged to get involved in other aspects of the organization beyond fundraising.*

Keep in mind, then, that what is most efficient for getting a job done thoroughly and quickly is rarely most effective for building an organization and developing new leadership. As you work on managing your volunteers, remember that you are ultimately trying to ensure that the organization could continue even if a key person were suddenly not available. By keeping your eye on the prize of longevity and stability of the organization, you will structure your volunteer management efforts much differently and will find that, even today, there are plenty of people who want to be active, engaged volunteers.